ZEN MIND
JEWISH MIND

KOAN, MIDRASH, & THE LIVING WORD

Rami Shapiro

Monkfish Book Publishi
Rhinebeck, New

Zen Mind Jewish Mind: Koan, Midrash & The Living Word Copyright © 2025 by Rami Shapiro

All rights reserved. No part of this book may be used or reproduced in any manner without the consent of the publisher except for in critical articles or reviews. Contact the publisher for information.

Paperback ISBN 978-1-958972-65-6
eBook ISBN 978-1-958972-66-3

Library of Congress Cataloging-in-Publication Data

Names: Shapiro, Rami M, author.
Title: Zen mind Jewish mind : koan, midrash, and the living word / Rabbi
  Rami Shapiro.
Description: Rhinebeck, New York : Monkfish Book Publishing Company, [2025]
Identifiers: LCCN 2024039825 (print) | LCCN 2024039826 (ebook) | ISBN
  9781958972656 (paperback) | ISBN 9781958972663 (ebook)
Subjects: LCSH: Judaism--Relations--Buddhism. |
  Buddhism--Relations--Judaism. | Spiritual life--Zen Buddhism. |
  Spiritual life--Judaism.
Classification: LCC BQ9269.4.J8 S53 2025 (print) | LCC BQ9269.4.J8
  (ebook) | DDC 296.3/9943--dc23/eng/20240904
LC record available at https://lccn.loc.gov/2024039825
LC ebook record available at https://lccn.loc.gov/2024039826

Book and cover design by Colin Rolfe

Monkfish Book Publishing Company
22 East Market Street, Suite 304
Rhinebeck, New York 12572
(845) 876-4861
monkfishpublishing.com

ZEN MIND

JEWISH MIND

For Jikan & Professor Unno

Jikan said, "The Great Way is not difficult for those without preferences."[1]

"Isn't preferring no preferences to preferences itself a preference?" I asked.

"Yes," Jikan said.

"Then isn't Zen built on a paradox?"

"Yes," Jikan said.

"What am I to make of this?"

"Zen is Jewish," Jikan said.

"What do you hope to achieve with your studies?" Professor Unno asked.

"I wish to be the Alan Watts of Judaism," I said.

"If you succeed, I have failed. If you fail, just maybe I have succeeded."

> [As an undergraduate I studied Buddhism with Taitetsu Unno, a Pure Land Buddhist priest and professor of Buddhist studies at Smith College in Northampton, MA. Professor Unno brought Joshu Sasaki Roshi to lead Zen retreats on campus. It was at these retreats that I first met Roshi and his *jikijitsu* or directing monk, the Jewish songwriter and poet Leonard Cohen whose Buddhist name was Jikan/Noble Silence. My conversations with Professor Unno and Jikan are reconstructed from memory.]

[1] Opening verse of the Chinese Chan/Zen poem *Hsin hsin ming*.

CONTENTS

Preface: No Boundaries, No Walls   ix

Introduction: Who Benefits?   xiii

PART ONE
NARROW MIND & SPACIOUS MIND

Chapter 1: Dharma Eye, God's I   3

Chapter 2: Dead Words, Living Words, One Word   8

Chapter 3: Koan and Midrash   19

Chapter 4: Original Nature   37

Chapter 5: The Yoga of Conversation   57

PART TWO
HOW TO

Chapter 6: How to Listen   73

Chapter 7: How to Speak   78

Chapter 8: How to See   82

Chapter 9: How to Eat	87
Chapter 10: How to Pray	95
Chapter 11: How to Love	105
Chapter 12: How to Fight	110
Chapter 13: How to Forgive	115
Chapter 14: How to Thank	120
Chapter 15: How to Rest	125
Chapter 16: How to Walk	134
Chapter 17: How to Wake Up (in the Morning)	139
Chapter 18: How to Shit	142
Chapter 19: How to Vote	145
Chapter 20: How to Die	153
Afterword: Zen Mind/Jewish Mind	159
Acknowledgements	161
About the Author	163

· PREFACE ·

NO BOUNDARIES, NO WALLS

You may be familiar with Shunryu Suzuki Roshi's *Zen Mind, Beginner's Mind*, a book I have read many times over the past half century and which provided the inspiration to Zen Mind, Jewish Mind.[1] According to Suzuki Roshi, Beginner's Mind is "empty, free of the habits of the expert, ready to accept, to doubt, and open to all the possibilities. It is the kind of mind which can see things as they are, which step by step and in a flash can realize the original nature of everything."[2]

The Jewish equivalent of Beginner's Mind is Questioning Mind. The Passover Haggadah speaks of Questioning Mind in the passage called The Four Children. Of the four, only the third, the Simple, demonstrates an authentic Questioning Mind.

The first two, the Wise and the Wicked, question the meaning of Passover and the rituals associated with it, but do so within the conventions of communal tradition differing only in that the Wise place themselves within the community, while the

---

[1] Shunryu Suzuki, *Zen Mind Beginner's Mind* (Shambhala Publications, 1970).
[2] Richard Baker, Introduction to Shunryu Suzuki, *Zen Mind Beginner's Mind* (Shambhala Publications, 1970), xiv.

Wicked place themselves outside the community. The Simple, on the other hand, asks a deeper and more existential question saying only, *Mah zeh*/What is this? The Questioning Mind of the Simple one is the Jewish equivalent of Suzuki Roshi's Beginner's Mind: "ready to accept, to doubt, and open to all the possibilities."

According to the kabbalists, Jewish mystics, the Hebrew word *Mah*, conventionally translated as "what," is a verbal sign standing in for the ineffable Name of God: YHVH, the Happening happening as all happening revealed to Moses in Exodus.[3] The connection of *Mah* and YHVH comes from *Gematria*, Hebrew numerology. When each letter of the four–letter Name YHVH is spelled out in full, the gematria of YHVH is 45: *yud/20 + hey/6 + vav/13 + hey/6*, the same numerical value as the word *Mah* (*mem/40 + hey/5*).[4] When words share the same numerical value they may be read as synonyms. Hence: *Mah* equals YHVH. The Simple One is not only asking "What is this?" but affirming "YHVH is this!" When we inquire into the nature of things with Beginner's Mind we discover that this and everything is YHVH.

Regarding the fourth child "who knows not how to ask" we are told to *patach lo*, to open the child to the art of questioning. Asking questions is key to Jewish Mind, the goal of which is to cultivate Questioning Mind.

Jewish Mind/Questioning Mind and Zen Mind/Beginner's Mind are the same mind: dynamic, daring, iconoclastic, often humorous, and devoted to shattering what Zen calls "dead words"—words, texts, isms, and ideologies closed to fresh inquiry.

Zen Mind, Jewish Mind is an expression of Zen Mind/Jewish

[3] Exodus 3:15.
[4] When YHVH is read simply as the four consonants Y, H, V, H, the numerical value of YHVH is 26.

Mind. It is not a scholarly study of anything, let alone Zen or Judaism, and, despite all the footnotes, rests solely on my fifty-plus years of playing in the garden of Judaism, Zen, and *advaita*/nonduality.

There once was a time—decades ago—when Judaism, Zen, and advaita were separate sections of this garden, walled off from one another by the rules of scholarship, religious strictures, and a concern not to violate the laws of cultural appropriation. That time is long past, and I no longer care about any of these things. As my Theosophical Society friends put it: *satyat nasti paro dharma*, "There is no religion higher than truth."

All I care about now is continually returning to Beginner's Mind, Questioning Mind, Zen Mind, Jewish Mind that asks *Mah zeh*: inquiring into everything and discovering the One Thing that manifests as all things.

• INTRODUCTION •

WHO BENEFITS?

What's the difference between religion and spirituality? Religion defines you; spirituality deconstructs you.

I often distinguish between religion and spirituality, and between faux spirituality and authentic spirituality. I do so by asking a single question of any religion or spiritual system: *cui bono*, or *who benefits?*

When asked about any religion, the answer is always the same: the beneficiaries of religion are the power elites who dominate the religion and control those who follow the religion.

This isn't surprising. Religion—any religion—is a hierarchical system of domination resting on untestable beliefs embodied in ritual and law, and enforced by a self-appointed leadership claiming to speak for whatever god or ultimate authority the religion represents.

The word "religion" comes from the Latin verbs *ligare* and *religare*, which mean "to bind" and "to connect." In this, *religion* is like the word *yoga*, with its root in the Sanskrit *yug*, "to yoke." At its best, religion reveals the connection between you and the greater reality of which you are a part, but religion is rarely at its best, and most often rests on the notion that you are *apart from* rather than *a part of* this greater reality. While religion promises to help you overcome the separation between you and the other, it never actually does so, blaming its failure to do so on you rather than on itself. As an ex-priest once said to me:

> This is the genius of religion: By the time you know the promise of salvation is a scam, it's too late— you're already dead. That's why the fulfillment of the promise is always in the afterlife or the next incarnation. If you're convinced that adhering to this or that religion can secure you a better berth in the afterlife or a better birth in the next life, you are going to turn your will and your wealth over to whoever is in charge. Religion is a con. You can't get right with God because there is no God!

I am sympathetic to this argument, but not to its conclusion. The real reason religion cannot fulfill its promise to bridge the gap between you and God isn't because there is no God, but because there is no gap, and the harder you try to overcome an imaginary gap, the larger you imagine the gap to be. It is your effort to overcome that makes overcoming impossible. To borrow from Master Lin-Chi, in Zen Mind/Jewish Mind "There is no place for using effort. Just be ordinary and nothing special. Eat your food, move your bowels, pass water, and when you are tired go and lie down. The ignorant will laugh at me, but the wise will understand."[1]

The "problem" with Zen Mind/Jewish Mind, as Lin-Chi defines it, is that there is no money in it. It empowers no clergy,

---

[1] Alan Watts, *Beat Zen, Square Zen, and Zen* (City Lights Books, 1959), 3.

establishes no hierarchy, and requires no financial obligation on the part of followers.

It is the failure of religion to fulfill its promise, and its obvious obsession with money and fear, that cause many people to abandon religion for spirituality. But here too there is a problem, which is why I make a distinction between faux spirituality and authentic spirituality—by once again asking *cui bono*: who benefits?

There is a tendency to assume that faux spirituality is any spiritual system to which the answer to the question *cui bono* is "the guru" or "the teacher." While you wouldn't be wrong to assume this, this isn't what I have in mind. When the answer to question *cui bono* is "the guru," "the teacher," "the prophet," "the medium," etc. you are dealing with what I call "religion lite" in that this is still a hierarchical power grab based on money and fear. What I call faux spirituality is more subtle and has nothing to do with power and fear. The answer to "who benefits" in faux spirituality is "ME."

Faux spirituality is all about you and your feelings, about getting what you want out of life, about fulfilling your hopes, dreams, and desires, about reducing stress and improving your looks, your relationships, and your finances. Faux spirituality is all about the worship of ME.

People who worship ME often talk about God's plan for their life. Here is a typical (and by no means rare) conversation I have had with one worshipper of ME.

> Worshipper of ME: "I'm struggling right now. My partner left me, and I'm between jobs. Paying the rent was impossible, so I moved back home with my parents, living in their partially finished basement. But I'm not panicking because I know God's all-powerful and in charge and he has a plan for my life."

Rabbi Rami: "How do you know God's plan isn't for you to be single, unemployed, and living in your parents' basement?"

WoM: "How could that be God's plan for me?"

RR: "How could it not be God's plan for you? It's what's happening to you right now. If God is all-powerful, as you say, and if God wanted something else for you, you would be doing something else. If God's in charge, and you're single, unemployed, and living in your parent's basement, this must be God's plan."

WoM: "I'm better than that. God wants more for me than that. Doesn't he?"

RR: "I don't know. But look at the millions of homeless, starving, war-ravaged humans in the world. Evidently this is God's plan for them. Compared to them, God's plan for you isn't so bad."

WoM: "Sure, but I'm not them...."

The conversation goes in circles, forever orbiting around ME. And so does faux spirituality. Whether it is yoga, dreamwork, mindfulness, kabbalah, manifesting, or almost any other spiritual practice on the market today, if the point is to celebrate ME, to feed ME, to entertain ME and elevate ME, then it is not authentic spirituality. Why? Because authentic spirituality has nothing to do with ME at all. As Alan Watts wisely observed:

Odd as it may sound, the ego finds that its own

center and nature is beyond itself. The more deeply I go into myself, the more I am not myself, and yet this is the very heart of me. Here I find my own inner workings functioning of themselves, spontaneously, like the rotation of the heavenly bodies and the drifting of the clouds. Strange and foreign as this aspect of myself at first seems to be, I soon realize that this *is* me, and much more than my superficial ego. This is not fatalism or determinism, because there is no longer anyone being pushed around or determined. There is nothing that this deep "I" is not doing. The configuration of my nervous-system, like the configuration of the stars, happens of itself, and this "itself" is the real "myself."[2]

This "deep I" is what Torah calls *Ehyeh*, the first-person singular form of the Hebrew verb *h-y-h*, "to be" or "to happen." Ehyeh is the first Name of God revealed to Moses at the Burning Bush: *Ehyeh asher Ehyeh*: the I'ing forever I'ing.[3] Ehyeh is the Divine I, infinite Consciousness, happening as all creation the way the ocean happens as all its waves. Ehyeh is the ocean; YHVH, the third-person singular form of the Hebrew verb *h-y-h* and the second Name of God revealed to Moses, is the waving we perceive as waves.

Ehyeh/YHVH is not a fixed entity, but a dynamic process of continual creation and destruction. When you read in the prophet Malachi, "I am YHVH, I do not change,"[4] you must remember that both "I am" and YHVH are verbs implicitly active and changing. Malachi is saying Ehyeh/YHVH doesn't change from one state to another, from "X" to "Y," or from on

---

[2] Watts, *Beat Zen, Square Zen, and Zen*, 6.

[3] Exodus 3:14.

[4] Malachi 3:6.

to off, because Ehyeh/YHVH is the process that includes "X" and "Y" and "on" and "off." Ehyeh/YHVH doesn't change because Ehyeh/YHVH *is* change. And this flow, this Ehyeh/YHVH, this deep "I" is you.

My experience of Ehyeh/YHVH is my experience of Tao and my experience of Sunyata, all four of which are Names for the source and substance of all reality. Lao Tzu puts it this way:

> All beneath heaven, the ten thousand things;
> it's all born of Presence,
> and Presence is born of Absence.

"It's important to understand here that Absence is not some kind of metaphysical dimension: it is instead simply the empirical Cosmos seen as a single generative tissue, while Presence is the Cosmos seen as that tissue individuated into the ten thousand distinct things constantly giving birth to new things."[5] Given my experience with Zen Mind/Jewish Mind, throughout *Zen Mind, Jewish Mind* I will use the albeit awkward formulation Ehyeh/YHVH/Tao/Sunyata when referring to Reality.

Zen Mind/Jewish Mind is the realization of the deep "I" and the momentary eradication of the surface ME. This eradication is what the Psalmist calls *kalta nafshi*, the obliteration of the separate self,[6] and the realization of what Buddhists call *anatta*, non-self.

All this should be understood in light of the ninth-century Ch'an master Qingyuan Weixin's teaching, "Before I studied Ch'an, I saw mountains as mountains and rivers as rivers. When my understanding deepened, mountains were no longer mountains, and rivers were no longer rivers. But now that

[5] David Hinton, *China Root: Taoism, Ch'an and Original Zen* (Shambhala Publications, 2020), 22.
[6] Psalm 84:3.

my study has ripened, I am at peace for once again mountains are mountains, and rivers are rivers." That is to say, authentic spiritual awakening doesn't eliminate the self, what I'm calling ME, it simply places it in its proper place. Mountains, rivers, and ME are not delusions to be eradicated, but illusions to be understood.

The difference is this: a delusion is something that doesn't exist, like a pink elephant appearing to a person in the throes of delirium. But an illusion is a misreading of something that *does* exist, like a magician making an elephant disappear from a stage. The elephant is real, and its disappearance is real. But how the elephant disappeared is not how the elephant appeared to disappear. ME is real as far as it goes; it just isn't as real as far as it pretends to go.

ME is a temporary expression of the infinite Ehyeh/YHVH/Tao/Sunyata happening as all happening, the way a wave is a temporary expression of an ocean waving. ME arises and falls, thinks and feels, and experiences sensations pleasant and unpleasant. ME is a natural phenomenon to be respected but not clung to.

It is clinging to ME that causes suffering. Why? Because ME is intrinsically *hevel*, impermanent.[7] Worse still, it is ME that is doing the clinging. This is like trying to smell your own nose or trying to point to your index finger with that same finger. It can't be done—and the more you try, the more frustrated you become, and the more *dukkah*, the Buddhist term for dissatisfaction, you create for yourself.

Faux spirituality is all about being special; authentic spirituality is all about being nothing special—or what the Chinese call *wu-shih*. Zen Mind/Jewish Mind perceives the nothing-special

---

[7] Ecclesiastes 1:2. Conventionally rendered "vanity," and "futility," *hevel* is better understood as "breath." "Humans are like mere *hevel*/breath" (Ps.144:3-4) and is meant to express impermanence.

quality of reality as the manifesting of Ehyeh/YHVH/Tao/Sunyata.

Cui bono? Who benefits from authentic spirituality? No one. Or maybe everyone. Or more accurately, the Only One who is everyone. But certainly not ME.

PART ONE

NARROW MIND & SPACIOUS MIND

· CHAPTER 1 ·

DHARMA EYE, GOD'S I

Long ago, I received an invitation to participate in an exercise in interfaith exegesis where participants received a text from a tradition not their own, about which they were to write a commentary drawn from their own tradition. The text I was to comment on came from Zen Master Dogen.

> To study the Buddha Way is to study the self; to study the self is to forget the self; to forget the self is to be actualized by myriad things. When actualized by myriad things, your body and mind as well as the body and mind of others drop away. No trace of realization remains and this no trace continues endlessly.[1]

Dogen's opening statement, *To study the Buddha Way is to study the self*, is a simple affirmation offered without evidence or

---

[1] Eihei Dogen, *Moon in a Dewdrop: Writings of Zen Master Dogen*, ed. and trans. by Kasuaki Tanahashi (North Point Press, 1995), 70.

argument. You either accept it as true or you reject it as false. If you reject it as false, there is no need to read the rest of what Dogen has to say. Since I find Dogen's teachings of immense value, I choose to accept his opening statement as true and see where it leads me.

His opening affirmation leads to two testable statements: *to study the self is to forget the self; to forget the self is to be actualized by myriad things.* My own experience with *zazen*, or Zen meditation—which is what I understand the phrase *study the self* refers to—does lead to a *forgetting of the self*: after a while, there is sitting, but no Rami doing it.

From a Jewish point of view, the reason for this forgetting is found in the story of the Burning Bush.

Moses is shepherding his father-in-law's flocks, as he has done for decades. This time, though, he notices a bush burning just off the sheep path. According to Jewish tradition, this bush was always burning, but Moses, focused as he usually was on sticking to the path, never noticed it before. Curious, Moses steps off the path and is confronted by the Voice of God: "Moses! Moses!" Moses replied, "*Hineni!* Here I am!"[2]

There is no encounter with the Divine until we are willing to step off the path of the comfortable, the safe, the conventional. This is not to say God is absent from the path—the bush was always burning—but that when we are attached to the path, we are oblivious to God.

Moses steps off the path and God calls his name twice. Why twice?

The first time, God speaks to Moses' *mochin d'katnut*, narrow mind, the mind or self that imagines itself to be apart from God. The second time, God calls to his *mochin d'gadlut*, spacious mind, the Self that knows itself to be a part of God. It is only

[2] Exodus 3:4.

from spacious mind that Moses responds with *"Hineni!* Here I am." If Moses is to understand what God is about to reveal to him, he must do so from spacious mind rather than narrow mind.

God then gives Moses his first commandment: "Remove your sandals from your feet, for the place upon which you stand is holy ground."[3] Sandals are a human artifact designed to buffer the person from the harshness of the planet. God demands there be nothing between the earthling and the earth, just as there was nothing between the first earthling, *adam*, and the earth, *adamah*, in the creation story found in chapter two of Genesis.[4] This unity of earthling and earth is a prelude to the unity between human and God that is about to be revealed to Moses (and us) as the story continues.

Moses removes his sandals, and God charges him with returning to Egypt and liberating the Hebrew people from enslavement to Pharaoh. Realizing that he has been absent from Egypt for most of his life—and very much doubting that anyone will take him seriously when he claims to have encountered God—Moses inquires as to God's Name, which is another way of asking, *What is the nature of divinity?* God replies, *"Ehyeh asher Ehyeh…* Tell the people *Ehyeh* has sent you…"[5]

Ehyeh is not a name or a proper noun, but a verb, the first-person imperfect singular form of the Hebrew verb *h-y-h*, "to be." Ehyeh is the unmanifest, formless, and eternal *I'ing* of the universe. The reason *studying the self* leads to *forgetting the self* is that when you look deeply into the self—the narrow self imagining it is other than Ehyeh—this self disappears, and only Ehyeh remains. The self is simply a temporary formation of Ehyeh, the way a wave is a temporary formation of an ocean.

[3] Exodus 3:5.
[4] Genesis 2:7.
[5] Exodus 3:14.

This is what God reveals to Moses at the burning bush: There is only one Ehyeh, one eternal I that includes your temporal I, one eternal Self that includes your temporal self.

As soon as God says, "Say this to the Children of Israel, 'Ehyeh has sent me to you,'" God offers a second name, the ineffable YHVH. YHVH, too, is not a noun or proper noun, but the third-person imperfect form of the Hebrew verb "to be." Where Ehyeh is the eternal Subject, the Seer that cannot itself be seen, YHVH is the eternal object that one sees as the myriad forms of being. In Hinduism, Ehyeh is *Nirguna Brahman*, God without form, and YHVH is *Saguna Brahman*, God as all form.

This is what is revealed to Moses: God is all reality: the formless and the formed, the One and the many. When you study any form, in Dogen's case the form called "self," you forget the self, in that you move from YHVH to Ehyeh, realizing that YHVH is an extension of Ehyeh the way waving is an extension of the ocean. In this way, you "are actualized by myriad things," which is to say you see all things as Ehyeh/YHVH.

The rest of Dogen's teaching flows naturally from this realization: *When actualized by myriad things, your body and mind as well as the body and mind of others drop away* because they are all seen as Ehyeh/YHVH. There is nothing but I'ing, and *no trace of realization remains* because no trace of ignorance remains, either—for realization and ignorance are both Ehyeh/YHVH. And *this no trace continues endlessly* because realization and nonrealization are both erased.

Since everything is Ehyeh/YHVH, *samsara* and *Nirvana* are Ehyeh/YHVH. Since everything is Ehyeh/YHVH, then form and emptiness are Ehyeh/YHVH.

> I, unmanifested, am the total potentiality, the abso-
> lute absence of the known and the knowable, the

absolute presence of the unknown and the unknowable. I, manifest, am the totality of all phenomena, totality of the known in the inconceivability of the unmanifested unknown. There can be only I—the eternal I—totally unconditioned, without the slightest touch of any attribute, pure subjectivity... Let the ME disappear and immediately and spontaneously, you are I.[6]

You can't make the ME disappear, but you can invite it to disappear. Zen Mind/Jewish Mind is an invitation to disappear. You can do this in many ways, including zazen, chanting, laughter, love-making, and—as you will see in the chapters to come—wordplay.

---

[6] Ramesh S. Balsekar, Pointers from *Nisargadatta Maharaj* (The Acorn Press, 1982), 192.

• CHAPTER 2 •

DEAD WORDS, LIVING WORDS, ONE WORD

Dead words are to living words what a menu is to a meal. In this way, they have their place: a menu can point to a reality beyond itself, and when used as a pointer can be quite convenient. But dead words become problematic when the menu replaces the meal. When they do, as the Zen scholar D.T. Suzuki wrote,

> we leave life itself and involve ourselves in every kind of "logical" controversy. We construct our own traps and then struggle to escape from them, and as long as we are what we are, we cannot get away from this dilemma.[1]

With all due respect to Professor Suzuki, I would amend his statement to read "as long as we are *what we think we are*, we cannot get away from this dilemma." Our dilemma—struggling to escape

[1] D.T. Suzuki, *Zen Buddhism: Selected Writings of D.T. Suzuki* (Doubleday Anchor Book, 1956), 253.

from being entrapped in traps of our own imagining—is the inevitable result of a misunderstanding of who we are. As long as we think we are separate entities—separate from one another and from nature and the cosmos as a whole—we feel alienated, alone, and are condemned to seek a way out of our supposed isolation.

But when we cease to think of ourselves this way—indeed, when we cease to think of ourselves at all and simply come to see what is, *koach mah* in Hebrew (a play on the word *chochma*, or wisdom) and *tathata* (suchness) in Sanskrit—we see that the isolated ME is a fiction. We see that reality is a dynamic nondual Happening happening as all happening; a birthless, deathless process called by many names—YHVH, Tao, Brahman, Dharmakaya, Consciousness, Mind, etc.

The work of Zen Mind/Jewish Mind is freeing ourselves from this dilemma. Our freedom consists not in our rejection of words in general, but in our ability to see through dead words and replace them with living words. As Harry L. Weinberg explains:

> We are so accustomed to "making sense" out of a philosophy or methodology or religion—meaning that we look for the logic in it—that if we find none, we dismiss it as nonsense. But the Zen Buddhists assert that if we stop attempting to use our symbolusing processes we can discover a new, and to them more reliable and truer, understanding of ourselves, the world around us, and our relationship to it. They continually stress that we blind ourselves to reality by our words. We confuse what we say about things with the things themselves. The words get in our eyes, the map blinds us to the "true" nature of the territory.[2]

[2] Harry L. Weinberg, *Levels of Knowing and Existence: Studies in General Semantics* (Harper & Brothers, Publishers, 1959), 236.

It is our confusion of the map with the territory—the menu with the meal—that keeps us from directly experiencing reality. What Martin Buber says of the living word "You" in the following paragraph can be said of all living words:

> The relation to the [living word] You is unmediated. Nothing conceptual intervenes...no prior knowledge and no imagination; and memory itself is changed as it plunges from particularity into wholeness. No purpose intervenes...no greed and no anticipation... Every means is an obstacle. Only where all means have disintegrated encounters occur.[3]

Dead words point only to themselves. Living words invite an intuitive grasping of nonduality, where "all opposites and contradictions are united and harmonized into a consistent organic whole."[4] Zen Mind/Jewish Mind prefers living words to dead words.

> The dead [words] are those that no longer pass directly and concretely and intimately on to the experience. They are conceptualized, they are cut off from the living roots. They have ceased, then, to stir up my being from within, from itself. They are no more what the masters would call "the one word" which when understood leads immediately

---

[3] Martin Buber, *I and Thou*, Walter Kaufman, trans. (Charles Scribner's Sons, 1970), 62-63.

[4] D.T. Suzuki, *The Essentials of Zen Buddhism: Selected Writings* (Greenwood Press, 1962), 154.

to the understanding of hundreds of thousands of other words or statements given by the Zen master.[5]

Zen Mind/Jewish Mind is concerned with "the One Word" (in Chinese, *yi chu tzu*) that reveals the suchness of things as they are. In the context of Zen Mind/Jewish Mind, the One Word is the inexpressible Ehyeh/YHVH/Tao/Sunyata:

> The tao that can be spoken is not Tao.
> The name that can be spoken is not YHVH.
> In the realm of the dead word,
> Tao and YHVH are living words.
> In the realm of the living words,
> Tao and YHVH are the One Word.

You can't express the One Word in conventional language. YHVH lacks vowels and is therefore literally unpronounceable. As Lao Tzu says, "the tao that can be spoken is not the eternal Tao."[6] What you *can* do is *realize* the One Word— Ehyeh/YHVH/Tao/Sunyata—happening in, with, and as this and every moment. You can then respond to this and every moment in a manner that shatters dead words by employing living words. Or, to put matters differently, you can tear up the menu and taste the meal.

Take, for example, Lin-Chi's *Kwatz!*:

> Master Lin-Chi (Rinzai) was persuaded to address the assembled monks. "If I were here to discuss the truth of Ch'an [Zen] I could not even open my mouth," Lin-Chi said, "but perhaps I can respond

[5] D.T. Suzuki, *Zen and Japanese Culture* (Princeton University Press, 1959), 7-8.
[6] *Tao Te Ching* 1.

to your questions." A monk asked, "What is the basic meaning of Buddhism?" Lin-Chi shouted, "*Kwatz!*" The monk bowed low. Lin-Chi said, "This fine monk is exactly the kind of fellow worth talking to!"[7]

The purpose of Lin-Chi's Kwatz! is not to convey information, but to shock us out of our reliance on words, so that we might experience the moment directly. As D.T. Suzuki points out:

> When we attempt to find meaning [in exclamations like Kwatz!], we are far away from the truth of Zen. We must penetrate into the mind itself as the spring of life, from which all these words are produced…[Kwatz!] must be understood…as the direct demonstration of life—no, even as life itself.[8]

What is true about the effable Kwatz! of Zen Mind is true about the ineffable YHVH of Jewish Mind. As the Chabad Rebbe Menachem Mendel Schneerson makes clear:

> The absolute reality of YHVH, while extending beyond the conceptual borders of "existence," also fills the entire expanse of existence as we know it. There is no space possible for any other existences or realities we may identify—the objects of our physical universe, the metaphysical truths we contemplate, our very selves do not exist in their own

---

[7] Burton Watson, *The Zen Teachngs of Master Lin-Chi* (Columbia University Press, 1997), 9. My retelling.

[8] Suzuki, *Essays in Zen Buddhism*, 301.

reality; they exist only as an extension of divine energy...[9]

What Schneerson says of the nature of the universe in terms of YHVH finds its ancient parallel in the teaching of the second-century CE Indian Buddhist saint Nagarjuna, who opens his *Treatise on the Middle Way* with Eight Negations:

> All things arise contingent on all other things, hence each thing is of itself unborn and undying; beyond annihilation and yet impermanent; neither coming into existence nor going out of existence; and lacking both unity and self-identity. In this way, reality is free from all conceptual linguistic construction.[10]

Nagarjuna would agree with Rabbi Schneerson that "the objects of our physical universe, the metaphysical truths we contemplate, our very selves...do not exist in their own reality"; and Schneerson would agree with Nagarjuna that "each and every thing, no matter how refined, lacks its own intrinsic nature, i.e., it lacks intrinsic existence."[11] Schneerson speaks of this in terms of YHVH; Nagarjuna speaks of it in terms of *sunyata*: emptiness or nothingness.

Ehyeh/YHVH/Tao/Sunyata is unborn, undying, and beyond annihilation, yet the myriad forms it takes are impermanent; Ehyeh/YHVH/Tao/Sunyata neither comes into existence nor goes out of existence though the myriad forms it takes

---

[9] Menachem Mendel Schneerson, *Toward a Meaningful Life*, Simon Jacobson, ed. (William Morrow, 1995), 215.
[10] My rendition.
[11] Paul Williams, foreword to C.D. Sebastian, *The Cloud of Nothingness: The Negative Way in Nagarjuna and John of the Cross* (Springer, 2016), ix.

do both; and Ehyeh/YHVH/Tao/Sunyata, being nondual, embraces and transcends all notions of unity and diversity.

YHVH/Sunyata permeates all of space/time. YHVH/Sunyata is the only reality, and all beings are manifestations of YHVH/Sunyata. Any sense of independent existence is illusory, for "the divine essence is the one and only true reality."[12] As Torah puts it: "*ein od milvado*: there is nothing other than That, nothing other than YHVH."[13]

I have been teaching this idea for decades and can attest to how difficult it is for people to grasp. The problem is intrinsic in the act of teaching itself: teaching relies on language, and language supports the illusion of dualism:

> With the help of language, we always seek to express things in terms of their identity as if they had an intrinsic nature of their own.... The sole aim of Nagarjuna [and Zen Mind/Jewish Mind], it seems, is to free the human mind of the net of conceptualization and its corollary verbal proliferation...for what is ultimately real is *beyond concepts and language*.[14]

The Hebrew root *d-v-r* is used for "word," "speech," and "thing": the spoken word supports the illusion of the existence of separate things. From the perspective of Zen Mind/Jewish Mind, when we say something exists, we mean that it exists as a form of YHVH, which is nondual existence itself. It does not exist separate from YHVH, for there is nothing other than YHVH.

---

[12] Rachel Elior, *The Paradoxical Ascent of God: The Kabbalistic Theosophy of Habad Hasidism* (SUNY Press, 1993), 49-50.

[13] Deuteronomy 4:35.

[14] C.D. Sebastian, *The Cloud of Nothingness: The Negative Way in Nagarjuna and John of the Cross* (Springer, 2016), 70-71, italics in the original.

> [W]e must always pay careful attention to the sense of the word "exist".... We might mean *exist inherently*, that is, in virtue of being a substance independent of its attributes, in virtue of having an essence, and so forth, or we might mean *exist conventionally*, that is to exist dependently, to be the conventional referent of a term, but not to have any independent existence. No phenomenon, Nagarjuna [and Schneerson] will argue, exists in the first sense. But that does not entail that all phenomena are nonexistent tout court. Rather, to the degree that anything exists, it exists in the latter sense, that is, nominally, or conventionally.[15]

In other words, things exist as an extension of Ehyeh/YHVH/Tao/Sunyata in the way waves exist as an extension of the ocean that waves them. Ocean and wave are not two; they are nondual.

Nondual is a richer term than *oneness*, since *oneness* implies otherness. But nondual—advaita, not two—embraces the one and the other in a greater whole called, in Hebrew, *shlemut*. *Shlemut* embraces and transcends all duality in the way a magnet embraces and transcends the duality of its positive and negative poles. The difference between these poles is not erased in the magnet—indeed, their difference is an essential quality of the magnet. Rather, the magnet is a greater unity that includes their duality. As the founder of Hasidic Judaism, the Baal Shem Tov (1698-1760) observed:

> When we say "YHVH is One" we mean that

---

[15] Jay Garfield, *The Fundamental Wisdom of the Middle Way: Nagarjuna's Mulamadhyamakakarika* (Oxford University Press, 1995), 90.

ZEN MIND JEWISH MIND • 16

> nothing other than YHVH exists in all the universe. It is thus written, "The whole earth is filled with God's glory."[16] The main idea is that you should consider yourself as absolutely nothing. You should realize that you have no essence other than divine energy and that you are a part of the infinite YHVH. Therefore, nothing exists in the world except the absolute Unity which is YHVH.... There is therefore absolutely nothing that is devoid of Divine essence.[17]

This is what the prophet Isaiah reveals when God says, *Ani YHVH, ein od/I am YHVH, there is nothing else.*[18]

To see the depth of Isaiah's teaching, one needs to know a bit of Hebrew. The Hebrew word *ani*, "I," is spelled with three Hebrew letters: *alef-nun-yud*. The Hebrew word *ein*, "nothingness," is spelled with the same three Hebrew letters in a slightly different order: *alef-yud-nun*. The letter *yud* stands for the word *yadah*/consciousness. When your consciousness is focused outward, as it is in the word *ani*, you have a sense of self, an "I." When your consciousness is focused inward, as it is in the word *ein*, the "I" disappears into the infinite no-thingness of YHVH.

The eighteenth-century mystic Levi Yitzchak of Berditchev wrote:

> Those whose gaze is fixed on *ein* (no-thingness)... those who meditate on *ein*, their intellect, their *ani* is temporarily obliterated.... When they return from

---

[16] Isaiah 6:3.

[17] Baal Shem Tov, *Likutum Yekarim* 14d, cited in Areyeh Kaplan, *The Light Beyond* (Maznaim Publishing, 1981), 37, adapted for inclusivity and clarity.

[18] Isaiah 45:5.

17 • DEAD WORDS, LIVING WORDS, ONE WORD

such contemplation they find the essence of their intellect, is filled with the fullness of YHVH.[19]

Fixing your gaze on *ein*/nothing is, I suspect, like the practice of wall-gazing taught by Bodhidharma, who is said to have spent nine years sitting in meditation in front of a wall. Bodhidharma's biographer Tao-hsuan saw wall-gazing, or what he called wall-examining, as central to Bodhidharma's Zen: "[Q]uieting mind is wall-examining."[20]

I admit to finding wall-gazing enjoyable, but quieting my mind has never been a goal of my meditation practice. I simply wish to know—not just intellectually, but palpably—that all reality is "nothing but the One Mind [YHVH/Tao/Sunyata] besides which nothing exists.[21] Because this is so, there is no goal to be reached. As Huang Po taught:

> [The notion] that there is nothing which can be attained is not idle talk; it is the truth. You have always been one with the Buddha, so do not pretend you can attain to this oneness by various practices. If, at this very moment, you could convince yourself of its unattainability, being certain indeed that nothing at all can ever be attained, you would already be Bodhi-minded. Hard is the meaning of this saying! It is to teach you to refrain from seeking Buddhahood, since any search is doomed to failure.
>
> Bodhi (knowledge of the Buddha-nature) is no state. The Buddha did not attain to it. Sentient

---

[19] *Kedushat Levi* 176, my rendition. See Moshe Idel, *Absorbing Perfections: Kabbalah and Interpretation* (Yale University Press, 2002), 66.

[20] Jeffrey Broughton, *The Bodhidharma Anthology: The Earliest Records of Zen* (University of California Press, 1999), 66.

[21] John Blofeld, *The Zen Teachings of Huang Po* (Dutton, 1970), 29.

beings do not lack it. It cannot be reached with the body nor sought with the mind. All sentient beings are already of one form with Bodhi. If you know positively that all sentient beings are already one with Bodhi, you will cease thinking of Bodhi as something to be attained.[22]

---

[22] Blofeld, *The Zen Teachings of Huang Po*, 83.

• CHAPTER 3 •

KOAN AND MIDRASH

The iconoclastic nature of Zen Mind/Jewish Mind uses words "to tease mind past the realm of words, thereby returning mind to its original empty nature."[1] In Jewish terms I would put it this way: Zen Mind/Jewish Mind uses words to undermine *mochin d'katnut*, the narrow mind of self attached to dead words, to awaken *mochin d'gadlut*, the spacious mind of Self at home with living words. In so doing Zen Mind/Jewish Mind "cuts the ground from under one's feet and sweeps away the discursive structure patiently erected" by narrow mind.[2]

This is not to say that Zen Mind/Jewish Mind does away with words—it doesn't. What it does do is subvert narrow mind's tendency for taking words literally by dismantling "all our human conceptual constructions, all the explanations and

---

[1] David Hinton, *China Root: Taoism, Ch'an, and Original Zen* (Shambhala, 2020), 41.

[2] Bernard Faure, *The Rhetoric of Immediacy: A Cultural Critique of Chan/Zen Buddhism* (Princeton University Press, 1991), 312.

assumptions that structure consciousness and orient us and define us as centers of identity?"[3]

Because language arises from and reflects the original source of the cosmos,[4] language can be used to return us to our original nature. The problem with words isn't words per se, but the fact that they become reified, fixed, and dead.

The work of Zen Mind/Jewish Mind is to turn from dead words to living words, and in this way reawaken to the One Word that is our true nature: Ehyeh/YHVH/Tao/Sunyata.

One powerful method for doing this is wordplay. In the realm of Zen Mind/Jewish Mind, wordplay is not merely clever. And it must never be premeditated. Rather, it is spontaneous and effortless, the way a bell's response to its clapper is spontaneous and effortless.

In the context of a Zen *mondo* (dialogue) or a rabbinic *shaylah/shuvah* (question/response), the only acceptable answer is one that arises from the immediacy of the moment and speaks, albeit often obtusely, to a "trans–rational insight or the intuitive perception of truth."[5] The goal isn't so much to answer the question posed, but to invite the questioner to step beyond the question and experience the immediacy of the moment in which the question is asked: to shift from mah zeh?/What is this? to Mah Zeh!/YHVH is this! This invitation oft comes by means of koan and midrash.

A koan is a Zen anecdote "that seems or is nonsensical and is used to disrupt unnecessary dualistic discursiveness.... One of the purposes of using koans is to disrupt discursiveness in such a way that thought processes stop, then return to what is essential (like dwelling in mind) or morally important. In the

---

[3] Hinton, *China Root*, 1.

[4] Psalm 33:6: "By the word of YHVH the heavens were made, by the breath of God's mouth, the cosmos was born."

[5] Conrad Hyers, *Zen and the Comic Spirit* (Westminster Press, 1973), 154.

Zen tradition, such disruptions are used as tools to help students toward awakening."[6]

I was taught to turn a koan repeatedly in my mind the way Ben Bag Bag urged me to turn a passage of Torah: "Turn Her, and turn Her, for everything is in Her. Reflect on Her and grow old and gray with Her. Don't turn away from Her, for nothing is better than Her."[7] The purpose of turning koan and Torah is the same: to shatter dead words and the predetermined ways of viewing the world they support, and to see what is rather than what we are conditioned to see.

> When you want to come up with new ideas in your understanding of Torah, you must…take one verse or subject and review it many times, hammering on the door until it is opened for you.[8]

The same can be said of koan, where this hammering shatters "the ordinary dualistic meaning of letters and words" and reveals Buddha-nature.[9] In this way koan "are a means of resolving what is the most fundamental question of Ch'an practice, and perhaps for human consciousness in general: how to move past the illusory separation between consciousness and Cosmos."[10]

Koan and midrash undermine the verbal structures of your normative dualistic worldview. They free you to act

---

[6] Pamela Ayo Yetunde, *Casting Indra's Net: Fostering Spiritual Kinship and Community* (Shambhala, 2023), 78.

[7] *Pirke Avot*, 5:26. Torah is feminine in Hebrew and Her pronouns are "Her" and "She." Torah should never be referred to as "it."

[8] Reb Nachman of Breslov, *Sichoth HaRan 58*, cited in Aryeh Kaplan, *The Light Beyond*, 256.

[9] Lucien Stryk and Takashi Ikemoto, *Zen Poems of China and Japan: The Crane's Bill* (Grove Press, 1987), xix.

[10] Hinton, *China Root*, 115.

unselfconsciously in tune with the needs of the moment. In Zen, *zazen* (Zen meditation) is where the koan is turned; *sanzen* or *dokusan* (a meeting with the Zen master) is where the result of your turning is demonstrated.

The goal of sanzen isn't to answer the koan. The answers to most koan are known in advance.[11] The point is to embody the answer. This cannot be done through normal ways of thinking, since all conventional thinking is tied to dead words, and hence locked in the illusion of dualism.

Turning the koan over and over, you are brought to a point of mental exhaustion where conventional language is shattered, and the living word is manifest. "Koan training comes to its conclusion in the stage of perfect naturalness of freedom in both the absolute and the relative worlds…"[12]

Let me share one personal example from my own koan turning.

When I sat across from Joshu Sasaki Roshi for the first time in sanzen, he was holding a long, gnarled stick, which he pounded repeatedly on the hardwood floor. He asked me in his very limited English, "Where is God when stick hit floor?"

I said, "Ah…God is here?"

Roshi said, "More zazen" and rang a bell announcing my return to the zendo to reconsider my answer.

In the days that followed, I did this repeatedly, testing each new insight in sanzen, and getting the same response: "More zazen." It was a Sisyphean task; there was no way I was going to roll that koan up the hill to satori.

Until there was. I had a plan.

If you've worked with koan, you know that having a plan is not the same as responding to a koan, and putting your plan into

---

[11] Two major koan collections studied by students of Zen, *Bluff Cliff Records* and *Mumonkan*, for example, contain the answers to the koans.

[12] Alan Watts, *The Way of Zen* (Vintage Books, 1957), 169.

action with your roshi is doomed from the start. Here's what I planned to do: Sitting across from Roshi as the stick descended to the floor, I would grab the stick, yank it out of Roshi's hand, and shout, "No stick! No floor! Just God!" That was the plan. Here's what happened.

I sat across from Roshi. The stick descended to the floor. I grabbed the stick. I yanked the stick. Roshi didn't let go. He also did some Aikido move that sent me flying over his shoulder and landing hard on my back on the wood floor. The bell rang. Roshi said flatly, "More zazen."

I had nothing left to turn. I went back to my cushion to sit. And stewed. I settled into the routine of sitting, stewing, meditating while walking, stewing, and stewing some more.

I don't know how much time passed before I heard the bell summoning me to sanzen. Moments later I found myself sitting across from Roshi once again.

I had no idea how I got there, and no idea what to do now that I was there. I just watched as the stick descended to the floor and listened as Roshi said, "Where is God when stick hit floor?"

What happened next happened without me, and what I share with you here is a reconstructed memory. As the stick struck the floor, I clasped my hands together, raised my arms over my head, and slammed my body prostrate on the floor to Roshi's left, screaming "God is here!" I sat back up in front of Roshi and waited. And I blushed.

I had *become* the stick. You don't get more Zen than that. Seriously. I became the stick. I hit the floor. Not *like* the stick, but *as* the stick.

Roshi laughed. "Good answer!" he said. "Seventy-five percent. More zazen."

"You blushed," Jikan said later when I related my experience to him. "That cost you twenty-five percent."

As I recall, there is no blushing in midrash.

The Hebrew word *midrash* comes from the root *d-r-sh*, meaning "to search" or "to investigate." Midrash is an investigation of Hebrew scripture in search of inner meaning. While this is one understanding of the term, it is not the one used in the context of Jewish Mind.

To use midrash to uncover meaning intrinsic to Torah would make Torah a fixed text, something midrash and Jewish Mind refuse to do. As Talmud scholar Jacob Neusner wrote, the ancient masters didn't "write *about* scripture, they wrote *with* Scripture":

> Scripture supplied the syntax and grammar of their thought.... Scripture served as testimony and testament. It accomplished important purposes in the formation and expression of a larger, wholly cogent statement. But it constituted a subordinated and merely instrumental entity; not the court of last appeal and final judgment, not the ultimate source of truth and validation, except—of course—after the fact...Scripture formed a dictionary, providing a vast range of permissible usages of intelligible words. Scripture did not dictate the sentences that would be composed through the words found in that [limited] dictionary. Much as painters paint with a palette of colors, authors wrote with Scriptures. The paint is not the picture.[13]

From the perspective of Jewish Mind, a fixed Torah is a compilation of dead words: "an echo of greater truths that had been cut off from the divine to be ravaged by history and

---

[13] Jacob Neusner, *The Midrash: An Introduction* (Jason Aronson, 1990), x-xi.

repeatedly reconstructed by devoted human hands. In many early rabbinic traditions, indeed, the biblical text is identified not only as a dead form of sacred revelation pruned from an inexhaustible living branch of divine truth but also as a potentially deadly form of revelation"[14] leading people away from living words and locking them into dead words.

Jewish Mind reads Torah not as a narrative whole, but in fragments: verses, words, and letters taken out of context that can be used as catalysts for human creativity. "The verses of the Bible function for the rabbis much as do words in ordinary speech…. [They] can be recombined into new discourse, just as words are recombined constantly into new discourse."[15] In this way, the Torah "presents itself to the midrashic interpreter as a global corpus, a vast labyrinth of meaning in which all paths are possible."[16]

> Torah is a living organism animated by a secret life which streams and pulsates below the crust of its literal meaning; every one of the innumerable strata of this hidden region corresponds to a new and profound meaning of Torah. Torah, in other words, does not consist merely of chapters, phrases and words; rather is it to be regarded as the living incarnation of the divine wisdom which eternally sends out new rays of light….Each configuration of letters in it, whether it makes sense in human speech or not, symbolizes some aspect of God's creative

---

[14] Rebecca Scharbach Wollenberg, *The Closed Book: How the Rabbis Taught the Jews (Not) to Read the Bible* (Princeton University Press, 2023), 2.

[15] Daniel Boyarin, *Intertexuality and the Reading of Midrash* (Indiana University Press, 1994), 28.

[16] Betty Roitman, "Sacred Language and Open Text," in *Midrash and Literature*, eds. Geoffrey Hartman and Sanford Budick (Yale University Press, 1986), 160.

power which is active in the universe. And just as
the thoughts of God, in contrast to those of man,
are of infinite profundity, so also no single interpretation of Torah in human language is capable of
taking in the whole of its meaning.[17]

But if verses, words, and even letters can be recombined
into new affirmations, new teachings, and new truths, how are
we to determine which if any of these new combinations is true?

Enter the genius of Jewish Mind: you don't.

Where Zen Mind pushes you beyond the limits of language
by invoking the startled silence evinced by a shouted Kwatz!,
Jewish Mind pushes you beyond the limits of language by inviting a white noise of mutually exclusive and equally valued
teachings supported by the Jewish pedagogy of *elu v'elu*, "these
and these."

Rabbi Abba said in the name of Shmuel: For
three years, the School of Hillel and the School
of Shammai were in dispute. One said, "The law
should follow *our* view," and the other said, "The
law should follow *our* view." A heavenly voice
descended and declared: "*Elu v'elu divrei Elohim
Chayim*: These words [the opinions of the School of
Hillel] and these words [the opinions of the School
of Shammai] despite being mutually exclusive are
both the words of the Living God." Nevertheless,
the voice continued, "The law follows the opinion
of the School of Hillel."

The question then arose among the sages: If
all these words are the words of the Living God,

[17] Gershom Scholem, *Major Trends in Jewish Mysticism* (Schocken Books, 1971),
14.

why does the law follow the opinion of the School of Hillel? It is because the students of Hillel were gracious and humble in that they taught not only their own words but the words of the School of Shammai as well; indeed, they went so far as to consider Shammai's words before considering their own words.[18]

Elu v'elu is not about determining what is true in the context of a fixed Truth, but rather about creating a mind at home with the fluidity of truth.

How are we to answer those who complain saying, "How can I study Torah when Torah contains so many different and even contradictory opinions?" Say to them, all these opinions come from One God as it is written, "And God spoke *all* these words..." [19] [What matters] is not a unity of interpretations but the fact that we derive multiple interpretations from the one Torah and the One God.[20]

Before we go any further, look at how the verse "And God spoke all these words..." is used—or, rather, misused—in this teaching.

The verse comes from Exodus 20:1 and introduces the Ten Commandments. In the context of the chapter, "all these words" refers to all the words of the Ten Commandments found in Exodus 20:2-14. But the sages, employing Jewish Mind, lift the verse out of context and use it as an independent figure of speech. The fact that the phrase "all these words" has a specific

[18] Talmud, *'Eruvin* 13b.
[19] Exodus 20:1.
[20] Talmud, *Chagigah* 3b.

function in chapter 20 of Exodus is irrelevant. Indeed, to limit "all these words" to that function would be to render it dead. By liberating "all these words" from Torah Herself, the sages make the words living words again.

This is how Jewish Mind undermines the fixity of language and frees us from the fixity of thought that flows from it.

The rabbis' joyful defense of multiple and contradictory interpretations of Torah "speaks not to a single divine truth but to the fundamental elusiveness of truth. It says, in effect, that the truth of scripture cannot be determined because its possible interpretations are many, and an authoritative source for this opinion or that can almost always be found."[21]

The indeterminate nature of truth is reflected in the fluid nature of Jewish Mind and its welcoming of paradox and contradiction. To paraphrase Martin Buber, when reading Torah, you must "not believe anything a priori or disbelieve anything a priori." You must read aloud the words written in the book in front of you and hear the words you utter and allow them to reach you as they will. "Nothing is prejudged."[22]

When you read Torah with Jewish Mind, you read Torah with Beginner's Mind: "The mind of the beginner is empty, free of the habits of the expert, ready to accept, to doubt, and open to all the possibilities. It is the kind of mind which can see things as they are, which step by step and in a flash can realize the original nature of everything." [23]

My teacher Rabbi Mordecai Kaplan (1881-1983), founder of Reconstructionist Judaism, brought this home to me when

---

[21] David Kraemer, *The Mind of the Talmud: An Intellectual History of the Bavli* (Oxford University Press, 1990), 105.

[22] Martin Buber, *The Way of Response*, ed. N. Glatzer (Schocken books, 1966), 75, adapted.

[23] Richard Baker Roshi, *Introduction to Zen Mind, Beginner's Mind*, Shunryu Suzuki. Boulder, CO: 2020, p. xiv.

I went to visit him at his home in Jerusalem, shortly after I'd attended his ninety-fifth birthday party. I sat in his living room and waited nervously as the great sage slowly made his way down the stairs to sit in a large chair.

I had written my master's thesis on Reconstructionist Judaism and had shared a copy with him. I thought we were going to talk about my understanding of his philosophy. Instead, without any niceties, Rabbi Kaplan pointed to a large print Hebrew/English Bible and commanded me to read a particular passage of the prophet Jeremiah. I no longer remember which one, though I do remember how poorly I read it.

"Your Hebrew is terrible!" he said. "Read it again." I did. And then, at his insistence, a third time and a fourth. Rabbi Kaplan had me read it over and over, until I could have recited it from memory.

Still not satisfied, he said, "Forget the Hebrew; read it in English. You can read English, can't you?" I could and I did. But it was still not good enough.

"You can't even read English!" Rabbi Kaplan bellowed. "Give it to me!"

I handed him the Bible and he read the Hebrew—the same Hebrew I had just read over and over. But he changed the inflections in such a way that the meaning of the text was completely different from the text I had read.

He handed the Bible back to me and laughed. "Don't worry," he said, "Nobody can read Torah but me!" I had read the dead words of Torah printed on the page. He had read the living words of Torah "that are in our mouths and on our hearts."[24]

Zen Master Joko Beck experienced something similar with her piano teacher.

---

[24] Deuteronomy 30:14.

Many years ago I was a piano major at Oberlin Conservatory. I was a very good student; not outstanding, but very good. And I very much wanted to study with one teacher who was undoubtedly the best…. Finally I got my chance…. When I went in for my lesson I found that he taught with two pianos. He didn't even say hello. He just sat down at his piano and played five notes, and then he said, "You do it." I was supposed to play it just the way he played it. I played it—and he said, "No." He played it again, and I played it again. And again he said, "No." Well, we had an hour of that. And each time he said, "No." … In the next three months I played about three measures, perhaps half a minute of music…. I cried most of those three months. And at the end of three months, one day, he said, "Good." What had happened? Finally, I had learned to listen…. It's that kind of attention which is necessary for our Zen practice. We call it samadhi, this total oneness with the object.[25]

Joko Beck's listening wasn't to reproduce the unique playing of her teacher, but to produce her own unique playing. What is true of playing piano in Zen Mind is true of playing midrash in Jewish Mind. Jewish Mind sees Torah not as a fixed narrative to be replicated, but as a fluid field in which one's imagination is invited to play. The goal of this play, which we call midrash, is novelty and unpredictability.[26]

This goal is made all the more profound by the realization

[25] Charlotte Joko Beck, *Everyday Zen: Love & Work* (HarperSanFrancisco, 1989), 9-10.

[26] Max Kadushin, *The Rabbinic Mind* (Block Publishing Company, 1972), 24. Kadushin's prefers the term haggadic interpretation to midrash.

that "the letters of the Torah, by their shapes, combined and separated, swaddled letters, curved ones and crooked ones, superfluous and elliptic ones, minute and large ones, and inverted, the calligraphy of the letters, the open and closed pericopes and the ordered ones, all of them are the shape of God."[27] That is to say all of them are doorways that can be opened through wordplay to reveal the infinite manifestings of YHVH in, with, and as all things.

The point of midrashic play is not to find The Truth of Torah, but to use Torah as a gateway to Truth that surpasses Torah. You do this by discovering as many truths as you can in Torah—and in this way freeing your mind from fixed truths altogether. The very nature of a Torah scroll, written as it is without vowels, is designed for this purpose. To paraphrase Rabbi Bahya ben Asher (1255-1340), "A Torah scroll is written without vowels [because] a vocalized word is limited to its vocalization, but a word without vowels may be read in many ways both marvelous and sublime."[28] There is no one way to breathe life into Torah: "Moses, our master, had been given a way of reading the Torah in many fashions, which are infinite, and each and every way points to the inner wisdom."[29]

In essence, consonants are always at risk of comprising dead words. It is only when vocalized—that is, only when you breathe life into the letters as vowels—do the dead words become living words. But if the vowels you breathe are routine—that is, if you limit yourself to breathing the same vowels, and reading the same words over and over, then your breath becomes stale, and your words are once again dead.

---

[27] Moshe Idel, "Infinities of Torah in Kabbalah," in Geoffrey H. Hartman and Sanford Budick, *Midrash and Literature* (Yale University Press, 1986), 145.

[28] Moshe Idel, *Absorbing Perfections: Kabbalah and Interpretation* (Yale University Press, 2002), 86.

[29] Idel, *Absorbing Perfections*, 85.

To keep that from happening, Jewish Mind revels in deliberate and creative "misreading": reading Torah in ways that shatter the simple, surface, or literal meaning of the text.

To assist in this creative act, passages of Torah are often juxtaposed one with the other "to highlight their incompatibility," and trigger your creativity.[30] Because each insight is considered independent of any other, students are not required to reconcile differences among them. On the contrary, you demonstrate your creativity by offering numerous and mutually exclusive understandings of the same text, thus shattering any notion that the text is fixed or dead.

The Torah is fundamentally indeterminant, fluid, and open to change. Its words are living because the reading of them is living. Any given passage can spark a fresh interpretation every time it is read, even when it is read by the same person.[31]

Jewish Mind is molded by elu v'elu and its openness to indeterminacy and multiplicity of meanings. "It is this receptive attitude, that we discern the most subtle feature" of Jewish Mind.[32] One might be inclined to conclude that Torah lacks any truth, but this would be a profound misreading of the foundational point of Jewish Mind. It isn't that Torah lacks truth, but that Torah contains *all* truth.

> Because the Torah is the revealed word of God it is both intelligible and inexhaustible in its meaning. Indeed, for Jewish mystics, the Torah functions as a mystical lexicon in which each word, each letter of each word, reveals some esoteric secret to those who know how to decipher and comprehend the language of the revealed text. Moreover, because it is

[30] Kadushin, *The Rabbinic Mind*, 71.
[31] Kadushin, *The Rabbinic Mind*, 133.
[32] Kadushin, *The Rabbinic Mind*, 133.

God's wisdom it can, as the *Zohar* teaches, be simultaneously read and understood on many different levels, each of which is true and none of which cancels the truth of the other.[33]

Torah turning is the art of subverting dead words and awakening living words through radical deconstruction of the text. The ancient rabbis developed a host of literary techniques to protect the fluidity of the word. Here are samples of just three of them: *gematria*, *atbash*, and vowel substitution.

Gematria is the practice of reading a Hebrew text not as letters but as numbers. Hebrew lacks a separate set of numerals, and calls on the letters of its *alef-bet* to function as both letters and numbers. This allows any given word, phrase, or verse to be read as a mathematical sum as well as a literary statement.

According to the rules of gematria, any text with the same numerical value can be used to decipher another with that same numerical value. For example, take the opening verse of Genesis reads, "*Bereshit bara Elohim et ha-shamayim v'et ha'aretz/* When *Elohim* created the heavens and the earth." The Hebrew noun *Elohim* is usually understood as God. Usually, but not necessarily.

The gematria of Elohim is 86: *Alef*/1 + *Lamed*/30 + *Hey*/5 + *Yud*/10 + *Mem*/40. Applying the principle of gematria, Elohim can be replaced by any other word with the same numerical value, if doing so adds to our understanding of the verse. One possibility is the Hebrew noun *haTeva*, Nature: *Hey*/5 + *Tet*/9 + Bet/2 + Ayin/70 = 86. This enables us to read the opening verse of Genesis this way: "When Nature created the heavens and the earth." Clearly, this naturalist reading of Torah offers a profound challenge to the conventional supernaturalist one.

[33] Steven T. Katz, *Comparative Mysticism: An Anthology of Original Sources* (Oxford University Press, 2013), 71-72.

Which is true? From the perspective of elu v'elu, this question is irrelevant. Both are true for both are the words of the living God.

Atbash is a substitution cipher, in which any given letter of the Hebrew alphabet is replaced by its opposite letter. [34] For example, the letter *alef*, the first letter of the *alef-bet*, can be replaced by *tav*, the final letter of the *alef-bet*; the second letter, *bet*, can be replaced by the next-to-last letter, *shin*; hence the name of the practice: *at-bash*.

One example of atbash is used to interpret the term *mitzvah*, or "commandment." In Hebrew, mitzvah is spelled *mem-tzadi-vav-hey*. Applying atbash to the first two letters of mitzvah, *mem* and *tzadi*, the spelling of the word mitzvah then becomes *yud-hey-vav-hey*, the ineffable Name of God: YHVH, as revealed in Exodus 3:15. In other words, the commandments of God are God, and embodying the commandments reveals oneself as a manifesting of God.

Vowel substitution, our third example of midrashic play, rests on the fact that Torah was originally written without vowels, and the vowels we are taught to breathe into the printed text are a matter of convention rather than revelation.

Midrashic play encourages you to find unconventional readings of Torah by breathing alternative vowels into the text.

Case in point: Leviticus 19:18 "*Ve'ahavta l'ray-ah-cha kamo-cha/*And you shall love your neighbor as yourself." Noticing that the Hebrew word *ray-ah/*neighbor is spelled with the same letters (*resh* and *ayin*) as the Hebrew word *rah/*evil," the eighteenth-century Hasidic Rebbe Nachman of Breslov[35] turned the text to read, "You shall love your evil as yourself." Loving your evil is acknowledging and taking ownership of your dark

---

[34] An early use of atbash can be found in the Talmud, Sanhedrin 22a.

[35] Nachman of Breslov (1772-1810) was the great-grandson of the Baal Shem Tov, founder of Hasidic Judaism.

side. This is what Carl Jung would later call your shadow: those parts of yourself you reject, repress, and often project onto others, rather than own up to as a part of yourself. Building on Reb Nachman's reading of Leviticus 19:18, if you are to effectively "love your neighbor," you must take care to own your own dark side and not project it onto your neighbor.

I seriously doubt this is what the author of Leviticus 19:18 had in mind when writing this verse. But from the midrashic point of view, original intent is irrelevant. Martin Buber explains this with living words of his own:

> Time after time, the images must be broken; the iconoclasts ["smashers of images"] must have their way. For the iconoclast is the soul in us which rebels against having an image that can no longer be believed in, elevated above our heads as a thing that demands to be worshipped. In longing for a God, we try again and again to set up a greater, a more genuine and more just image, which is intended to be more glorious than the last and only proves the more unsatisfactory. The commandment, "Thou shalt not make unto thee an image," does not, of course, refer merely to sculptured or painted images, but to our fantasy, to all the power of imagination as well. But we are forced time and again to make images, and forced to destroy them when we realize that we have not succeeded. The images topple, but the voice is never silenced.... The voice speaks in the guise of everything that happens, in the guise of all world events; it speaks to all generations, makes demands upon us, and summons us to accept responsibility.... It is of the utmost importance not to lose one's openness. But to be open means not to

shut out the voice—call it what you will. It does not matter what you call it. All that matters is that you hear it.[36]

And the voice says, *Elu v'elu divrei Elohim Chayim*: these and these are the words of the living God.

Midrash and koan shatter the dead words and free the living words that express the One Word of Ehyeh/YHVH/Tao/Sunyata, and in so doing help you in "achieving self-annihilation (*kalta nafshi*) in that you should become as nothing, that is you should no longer conceive or feel any separate essence identified as me."[37]

This is what Dogen called "forgetting the self" and what Zen scholar Winston King calls the "negation of the separate-distinct I-awareness (separate and distinct from other persons and things)…[that] divides one from that living interactive harmony with the rest of creation that Zen [and Jewish Mind] seeks to achieve. And the koan is the prime device for doing this. With the attention and emotions totally concentrated on the koan, the sense of I-ness is obliterated.[38]

As the Baal Shem Tov says regarding this, "If joy is felt as two human bodies come together, how much greater must be the joy of this union in spirit!"[39]

---

[36] Martin Buber, *The Way of Response* (Schocken Books, 1971), 38-39.

[37] Rabbi Aaron ben Moses Horowitz ha-Levi, *'Avodat ha-Levi, I, Mi-Kets*, 58b, my translation.

[38] Winston King, *Zen and the Way of the Sword* (Oxford University Press, 1993), 22.

[39] Baal Shem Tov, *Keter Shem Tov*, 387b.

• CHAPTER 4 •

ORIGINAL NATURE

Your original nature, your truest Self, is Ehyeh/YHVH/ Tao/Sunyata: "[I]t is that which is living, dynamic, devoid of mass, unfixed, beyond individuality or personality—the matrix of all phenomena.[1] You can't *become* your original nature because you already *are* your original nature; you don't seek after your original nature, rather you live from your original nature. But how?

There are no laws or rules for being who you are. But there are practices for remembering who you are and in this living your truest Self. The daily recitation of vows or promises is one of these practices.

Sometime in the early 1990s, several Jews living as laypeople at Plum Village, Thich Nhat Hanh's Zen community in France, reached out to me and requested "something Jewish" they could use as part of their liturgical practice at the village. I had been taken with Thich Nhat Hanh's Order of Interbeing (*Tiep Hien* in Vietnamese)—a community of nuns, monks, and lay people

---

[1] Yasutani Roshi cited in Philip Kapleau, *The Three Pillars of Zen* (Anchor Books, 1989), 119.

who live lives committed to the Fourteen Mindfulness Trainings, which I took as an expression of what it is to live from one's original nature. Here is an abbreviated list of the trainings:[2]

Openness: Aware of the suffering created by fanaticism and intolerance, we are determined not to be idolatrous about or bound to any doctrine, theory, or ideology, even Buddhist ones.

Non-Attachment to Views: Aware of the suffering created by attachment to views and wrong perceptions, we are determined to avoid being narrow minded and bound to present views.

Freedom of Thought: Aware of the suffering brought about when we impose our views on others, we are determined not to force others, even our children, by any means whatsoever—such as authority, threat, money, propaganda, or indoctrination—to adopt our views.

Awareness of Suffering: Aware that looking deeply at the nature of our suffering can help us develop understanding and compassion, we are determined to come home to ourselves, to recognize, accept, embrace and listen to our own suffering with the energy of mindfulness.

Compassionate, Healthy Living: Aware that true happiness is rooted in peace, solidity, freedom, and

---

[2] Thich Nhat Hanh, *Interbeing: Fourteen Guidelines for Engaged Buddhism* (Parallax Press, 1987). See also www.orderofinterbeing.org/.

compassion, we are determined not to accumulate wealth while millions are hungry and dying nor to take as the aim of our life fame, power, wealth, or sensual pleasure, which can bring much suffering and despair.

Taking Care of Anger: Aware that anger blocks communication and creates suffering, we are committed to taking care of the energy of anger when it arises, to recognizing and transforming the seeds of anger that lie deep in our consciousness.

Dwelling Happily in the Present Moment: Aware that life is available only in the present moment, we are committed to training ourselves to live deeply each moment of daily life.

True Community & Communication: Aware that lack of communication always brings separation and suffering, we are committed to training ourselves in the practice of compassionate listening and loving speech.

Truthful and Loving Speech: Aware that words can create happiness or suffering, we are committed to learning to speak truthfully, lovingly and constructively.

Protecting and Nourishing the Sangha: Aware that the essence and aim of a Sangha is the practice of understanding and compassion, we are determined not to use the Buddhist community for personal power or profit—or to try to transform our community *into* a political instrument.

Right Livelihood: Aware that great violence and injustice have been done to our environment and society, we are committed not to live with a vocation that is harmful to humans and nature.

Reverence for Life: Aware that much suffering is caused by war and conflict, we are determined to cultivate nonviolence, compassion and the insight of inter-being in our daily lives and promote peace education, mindful mediation, and reconciliation within families, communities, ethnic and religious groups, nations, and in the world. We are committed not to kill and not to let others kill.

Generosity: Aware of the suffering caused by exploitation, social injustice, stealing, and oppression, we are committed to cultivating generosity in our way of thinking, speaking, and acting.

Right Conduct [for lay members]: Aware that sexual desire is not love and that sexual relations motivated by craving cannot dissipate the feeling of loneliness but will create more suffering, frustration, and isolation, we are determined not to engage in sexual relations without mutual understanding, love, and a deep long-term commitment made known to our family and friends.

Taking the Fourteen Mindfulness Trainings as my guide, I recast the wisdom of the Ten Commandments to create a set of core precepts of Jewish Mind—Ten Promises—that could be affirmed daily by the Jews of Plum Village and elsewhere:

Spirituality is a source of liberation. Aware of the suffering caused by enslavement to things and ideas, I promise to free myself from all addictions and compulsive behaviors, both material and spiritual.

God cannot be named. Aware of the suffering caused by gods created in our own image for our own profit, I promise to recognize all ideas of God as productions of human beings, bound by history and circumstance, and forever incapable of defining Reality.

God cannot be owned. Aware of the suffering caused by the misuse of God and religion in the quest for power, I promise to liberate myself from all ideologies that demonize others and to honor only those teachings that uphold the freedom and dignity of woman, man, and nature.

Remember the Sabbath. Aware of the suffering caused by slavish attachment to work, consumption, and technology, I promise to set aside a weekly Sabbath day for personal and communal freedom, creativity, and play.

Honor your parents. Aware of the suffering caused by old age, I promise to care for my parents to the best of my ability and to promote the dignity and well-being of all elderly people.

Do not murder. Aware of the suffering caused by the wanton destruction of life, I promise to cultivate responsibility for and gentleness toward all beings.

Avoid sexual misconduct. Aware of the suffering caused by sexual irresponsibility, I promise to honor human sexuality and never degrade it through fear, violence, ignorance, selfishness, or deceit.

Do not steal. Aware of the suffering caused by exploitation, injustice, theft, and oppression, I promise to respect the property of others, to work for the just sharing of resources, and to cultivate generosity in myself and my community.

Do not lie. Aware of the suffering caused by harmful speech, I promise to speak truthfully and with compassion, to avoid gossip and slander, and to refrain from uttering words that cause needless division or discord.

Do not covet. Aware of the suffering caused by endless desire, I promise to live simply, avoid debt, enjoy what I have before seeking to have more, and labor honestly and justly for what I desire.

Reciting the Fourteen Vows and/or the Ten Promises reminds you what it is to live from your truest Self. Notice I am deliberately avoiding any notion that these are rules, laws, or commandments. Nor are they suggestions or guides. They are manifestations of original nature, and reciting them—aloud in community or silently to yourself—is a way of holding a mirror to original nature and reminding (re-minding) narrow mind to the greater wholeness of spacious mind of which it is a part.

There is no reward or punishment attached to either the Fourteen Mindfulness Trainings or the Ten Promises. "One who rejects them is not struck down by lightning; one who elects them does not find hidden treasures. Everything seems to remain just as it was."[3] Things remain just as they are because they cannot be other than they are, moment to moment. The point of living these teachings isn't to change what is, but to see what is more clearly, and in this way to live unconditionally. As Martin Buber notes:

> In the unconditionality of your deed you experience your communion with God…. For one who is unconditioned, God is the closest, the most familiar Being that you, through your own action, realize ever anew…. Any deed, even one numbered among the most profane, is holy when it is performed in holiness, in unconditionality.[4]

This is so because your "relation" to God—Ehyeh/YHVH/Tao/Sunyata—is not a relation at all, but a seamless union. "No system of concepts, no foreknowledge, and no fancy intervene between" you and Absolute Reality…. No set purpose, no greed, and no anticipation intervene between I and Thou…. Every means is an obstacle. Only when every means has collapsed does the meeting come about."[5]

Reciting the Ten Promises is not a means or a technique but a reminder of what is already so. When you remember what is so, your actions align with the original nature of things. This is because the truth of your original nature

> is not in the sky that you might excuse yourself from living it by saying, "Who can ascend to the heavens and retrieve it for us?" Nor is it across the sea that

[3] Buber, *The Way of Response*, 188, adapted.
[4] Buber, *The Way of Response*, 30, adapted.
[5] Buber, *The Way of Response*, 49, adapted.

> you might excuse yourself from living it by saying, "Who can sail across the ocean and retrieve it for us?" On the contrary, Truth is very near to you. In fact, it is already in your mouth that you might speak it, and on your heart that you might live it.[6]

And anyone who tells you otherwise is lying.

> If your teachers claim Truth is in the sky, do they mean to say that birds will get there before you? If they tell you it is across the sea, do they mean to say that fish will get there before you? What nonsense! Truth is within you and around you.[7]

Living the truth that Zen Mind/Jewish Mind knows, the truth that all reality is a manifesting of Ehyeh/YHVH/Tao/Sunyata calls you to live a "unified life," [8] a life lived awake to Ehyeh/YHVH/Tao/Sunyata as the fundamentally ineffable and nondual "living tissue that is inexplicably generative in its very nature,"[9] and knowing "that the whole sense of existence rests in the oneness of the truthful life"—not as some abstract idea, but as "the oneness of the path, the oneness of the truthful human way, that recovers the unified in the world and in each thing: the path as the oneness of the world, as the oneness of each thing."[10]

The Ehyeh/YHVH/Tao/Sunyata is not "perceived and known" as an object is perceived and known, but rather "lived and done."[11]

[6] Deuteronomy 30:12-14, my translation.

[7] Gospel of Thomas, logia 3, my rendition.

[8] Jonathan Herman, *I and Tao: Martin Buber's Encounter with Chaung Tzu* (SUNY Press, 1996), 72.

[9] Hinton, *China Root*, 2.

[10] Herman, *I and Tao*, 83.

[11] Herman, *I and Tao*, 84.

Ch'an master Lin-Chi (810-866) calls one who lives from and embodies original nature a True Person of No Rank, a phrase he likely took from the Taoist sage Chuang Tzu.

> Lin-Chi sat before his students and said, "Here in this lump of flesh you call 'myself' is a True Person of No Rank, no title, no name, who constantly flits in and out the gates of your face. If there are any among you who can't see this for a fact, then look closer!" He then leaped from his chair, grabbed the closest monk, and said, "Speak! Speak!" Just as the startled monk was about to speak, Lin-Chi shoved him away shouting, "True Person of No Rank-what a piece of shit!" Lin-Chi then walked back to this room.[12]

A Person of No Rank is a person with a genuine understanding of Ehyeh/YHVH/Tao/Sunyata.

> [Such a person] should not become unduly preoc-cupied with the scriptures and tenets of Buddhism [Judaism, or any "ism"]. Nor with the rules of con-duct and devotional practices that are believed to lead one step by step along the path of spiritual advancement.... Indeed, we see him [Lin-Chi] fre-quently having to admonish his hearers when they pounce with too great zeal and expectation on some novel phrase or term in his own discourse. All such "words and phrases" are to be put aside, and the student is to look with and to understand, once and for all, there is no goal to strive for because it

[12] Watson, *The Zen Teachings of Master Lin-Chi*, 13, adapted.

has been won already, no place to be journeyed to because one is there right now.... Once they have done that, once they have experienced true enlightenment and broken through the barrier of ignorance in the undifferentiated realm of Emptiness [Ehyeh/YHVH/Tao/Sunyata], then nothing more will be required of them. They will be persons with "nothing to do," not idle, of course, since daily activities never cease, but pursuing no purposive goal, reaching out for no distant ideal, accepting all experience as it comes to them and no longer being pushed around or led astray by their surroundings.[13]

What qualities does one who lives this way exhibit? Torah lists thirteen: (1) YHVH/knowing the divinity of Self, (2) YHVH/knowing the divinity of Other, (3) *El*/creativity, (4) *Rachum*/compassion, (5) *Chanun*/grace, (6) *Erech apayim*/equanimity, (7) *Rav Chesed*/utmost kindness, (8) *Emet*/utmost truth, (9) *Notzer chesed la-alafim*/preserving kindness, (10) *Noseh avon*/forgiving deliberate harm, (11) *Fesha*/forgiving accidental harm, (12) *Chata'ah*/forgiving unforeseen harm, and (13) *Nakay*/cleansing yourself of delusion.[14]

Don't imagine these thirteen qualities are separate from one another—or from the One. They are the One manifest in the awakened heart. When you are awake to the One, you manifest these thirteen qualities. This teaching is found embedded in gematria, Hebrew numerology.

Several times each day observant Jews recite the *Sh'ma*: Hear O Israel, YHVH is our God, YHVH is One/*Echad*. In Hebrew, the word *echad* is spelled with three letters: *alef*, *chet*, *dalet*. The numerological values of each leter is 1, 8, 4, respectively. Added

---

[13] Watson, *The Zen Teachings of Master Lin-Chi*, xxiv-xxv.
[14] The rabbis derived these qualities from their interpretive reading of Exodus 34:5-7.

together, *echad*, one, equals thirteen. From this, the rabbis teach that the oneness of the Divine is articulated in thirteen qualities of godliness revealed in Exodus 34:5-7.

Let's investigate each quality in turn.

KNOWING THE DIVINITY OF SELF AND OTHER

The first two of the thirteen qualities is a repetition of the Name YHVH, the Happening happening as all happening, and speaks to the Divine as Self and Other. Think of YHVH YHVH in terms of an ocean and its waving. Each wave is unique and distinct, yet all waves are the waving of the same ocean. So, too, each happening in the universe is unique and distinct, yet all happenings are the happening of the same Divine Reality called YHVH.

YHVH is repeated twice to remind us that YHVH is not one thing or another, but all things and beyond all things.

The Spanish Kabbalist Abraham Abulafia (1240-91) spoke to the first YHVH when he wrote: "Behold you are God and God is you; and you are so intimately one with God that you cannot by any means be other than God, for you are God. See now that I, even I, am God. God is I and I am God."

The Hasidic master Levi Yitzchak of Berdichev (1740-1810) spoke to the second YHVH when he wrote:

> Where will I find You? Where will I not find You?
> Wherever I go: You! And wherever I stay: You!
> Just you, only You, again You, nothing but You!
> When something's good: You. When something's bad: You.
> East—You; West—You; South—You; North—You.
> In the sky: You; On earth: You. Above: You. Below: You.

Wherever I turn, wherever I go: You, You, only You.

CREATIVITY

When you know **YHVH** as both Self and Other, you unleash your innate holy creativity, *El*,[15] the third of the Thirteen Qualities: the creativity to be your true self. As Martin Buber observed:

> Every person born into this world represents something new, something that never existed before, something original and unique…. Your foremost task is the actualization of your unique unprecedented and never-recurring potentialities, and not the repetition of something that another, and be it even the greatest, has already achieved.[16]

COMPASSION AND GRACE

Rabbi Abraham Joshua Heschel wrote, "A religious person is a person who holds God and humanity in one thought at one time, at all times, [and therefore] who suffers harm [when harm is] done to others, whose greatest passion is compassion, whose greatest strength is love and defiance of despair."[17]

Compassion isn't an expression of sympathy or pity, but an act of love and defiance in the face of hopelessness and nihilism.

---

[15] *El* is another Hebrew name for God. Since this is the name used in Genesis 1 creation story, I understand it to be the name of divine creativity.

[16] Martin Buber. *The Way of Man according to the Teaching of Hasidism* (Vincent Stuart, 1963), 16.

[17] Abraham Joshua Heschel cited in *Walking with God in a Fragile World*, James R. Langford and Leroy S. Rouner (Rowman & Littlefield, 2002).

It is also a willingness to share in the suffering of others in such a way as to alleviate their suffering as best you can.

Compassion of this sort—*rachum* in Hebrew—is a creative act. It makes meaning out of hardship and purpose out of anguish. As such, it is an expression of *El*, the holy creativity that is released when you awaken the first two divine qualities of YHVH YHVH: knowing God as Self and Knowing God as Other.

While it is true that all reality is the happening of God, it is also true that this happening is beyond human understanding. As Torah tells us, the very nature of reality is *tohu va-vohu*: wild, fluid, chaotic, and outside your willful control.[18]

The suffering caused by the wildness of life isn't a bug, but a feature. When you seek to bend reality to your will, you fail. And when you fail, you experience suffering. And because you experience suffering in your own life, you can have compassion for those who experience suffering in their lives.

The compassion that is the fourth of the Thirteen Qualities is the capacity to engage life without reservation, to be present to whatever is—even when that "what is" causes you suffering.

Why would you want to do this? Because, when you can do this, you become fearless, and when you fear less, you love more. Fear is the opposite of love. Fear closes us down, while love opens us up. And when we are open, we can work with suffering to the benefit of self and other.

Without the ability to see what is so, you become trapped in a fantasy about what you wish were so. Then you can easily lose the ability to engage fully with life, using that creativity that is uniquely your own.

Grace, *chanun* in Hebrew, is the quality of living with

---

[18] Genesis 1:2.

EQUANIMITY

Life does what it does because the conditions are such that it can do nothing else. Equanimity is the capacity to engage with what is without becoming entrapped in a fantasy about what should be.

The Hebrew for equanimity is *erech apayyim*, literally "long nosed." Equanimity involves engaging with life without scrunching up your nose in anger or disgust. Achieving equanimity requires us to see things as they are. The parable of Job has relevance here. Job was an innocent and upstanding person who lost everything—his children, his business, and his health—as part of a bet God made with Satan, to see if Job can maintain equanimity in the face of horror. Job does—through the realization that everything is a happening of God. As he says to his wife, "Should we not accept the good and the bad from God?"[19]

Some people refer to this as the "patience of Job." But this isn't actually patience; it's equanimity. Indeed, Job isn't patient at all. He demands that God explain to him why the world is the way it is. God responds by peppering Job with questions designed to reveal to him—and, through him, to you and me— that reality is beyond the human categories of good and evil, just and unjust, right and wrong.

The surety and certainty we humans look for in life is a fiction. Life offers only *tohu va-vohu*: creative chaos. Our challenge isn't to make the world fit our ideas of justice and fairness, but to live our ideals of justice and fairness in a world that is largely indifferent to them.

[19] Job 2:10

As the parable of Job comes to an end, Job glimpses the truth that all beings are the happening of God. Job says, "In my flesh I see God,"[20] and realizes the first of the Thirteen Qualities: God as Self. He then quickly realizes the second, and sees God as Other. Job recognizes that everything in the cosmos, even dust and ash, is the happening of God. And in that realization, Job finds comfort.

Most English translations of the book of Job mislead us by having Job despise himself and cover his flesh with dust and ash. But in the original Hebrew, Job finds comfort in being dust and ash, because he knows that dust and ash are also God: "I have heard you with my ears; but now my eyes have seen you. Therefore I will be quiet, comforted that I am dust."[21] This knowing brings Job the gift of equanimity.

KINDNESS AND TRUTH

Soon after the destruction of the Temple in Jerusalem by Rome in the late first century, Rabbi Yochanah ben Zakkai and Rabbi Yehoshua were on their way out of the city. Seeing the ruins of the Temple, Rabbi Yehoshua exclaimed: "How awful for us, the place where we could atone for our failures lies in ruins." Rabbi Yochanan replied, "My friend, do not grieve. We have another, equally effective form of atonement." "What is this equally effective form of atonement?" asked Rabbi Yehoshua. "Acts of kindness," Rabbi Yochanan said, "For God has said 'I desire kindness not sacrifice, and knowledge of God rather than burnt offerings.'"[22]

Kindness atones for our failures because our failures are

---

[20] Job 19:26.

[21] See Job 42:6, Stephen Mitchell, *The Book of Job* (North Point Press, 1987), xxviii.

[22] Hosea 6:6; *Avot de Rabbi Natan*, chapter 4.

rooted in a lack of kindness. Kindness is, as Torah puts it, loving both your neighbor and the stranger as yourself.[23]

Of course, "self" here isn't *mochin d'katnut*—narrow, egoic mind, which pits self against other, but "Self," *mochin d'gadlut*—spacious mind, which knows self and other as part of the greater nonduality of YHVH. Loving in this context means honoring the dignity of neighbor and stranger as the manifesting of God, by treating them with consistent kindness.

Practicing kindness is a means of atonement—at-one-ment, because practicing kindness reveals the nonduality of all life in, with, and as God. This nonduality is the truth, *emet*, that is the eighth quality. When we manifest the attribute of truth and see all beings as manifestings of YHVH, we cannot help but treat all beings with utmost kindness. And as we treat all beings with utmost kindness, we can't help but see them and ourselves as a part of YHVH.

PRESERVING KINDNESS

Every day, all day, each of us turns to memory to remind ourselves of who we are and why we matter. This is neither good nor bad; it is simply what human beings do. Knowing that this is what we do, each of us must ask ourselves: *Which memories do I use to build the self I imagine myself to be?*

So, please—right now—ask yourself: *What memories are the building blocks of my life? What stories do I preserve? What stories do I tell and retell to anchor myself in my idea of myself? Do I remember kindnesses received? Do I remember hurts endured?*

Notzair Chesed la-Alaphim, preserving kindness for generations, is the act of remembering kindness rather than nursing

[23] Leviticus 19:18; 34.

grudges. By remembering and retelling acts of kindness, you help to create a self that is loving and kind.

FORGIVENESS

The tenth, eleventh, and twelfth qualities deal with three kinds of forgiveness (*nosay*): *avon, fesha,* and *chata'ah*: forgiving deliberate harm, forgiving accidental harm, and forgiving unforeseen harm.

Avon, deliberate harm, is the result of someone intentionally seeking to hurt you. *Fesha*, accidental harm, is the result of someone intentionally seeking to help themselves and inadvertently causing you harm. *Chata'ah*, unforeseen harm, is the result of someone intentionally seeking to benefit you, but who brings you harm instead.

Forgiving these three different forms of harm doesn't require you to forget the harm you experienced or excuse those who caused it. Instead, it calls you to move *through* your hurt, so that you no longer carry within you the anger that it generates.

True forgiveness is about freeing yourself from anger more than it is about making peace with other people. When the anger passes, reconciliation may happen, but it is the passing of anger that matters most.

Anger is an emotion and emotions, like most of reality, cannot be controlled directly by your will. So, how can we let go of anger? We can't let go of anger in the same way that we would let go of a clasped hand or a runner's baton. But we can allow our anger to fade by cultivating forgiveness. As one teacher (whose name escapes me) put it:

> Imagine you are out alone on a lake, canoeing. A fog rolls in and you decide to row to shore for safety's sake. As you do so, you notice another canoe

heading straight toward you. You assume that the fog is blinding the occupants of the other canoe to your presence, so you call out for them to turn aside. But the others don't respond. In fact, their canoe picks up speed as it draws closer to you. You begin to panic. No matter which way you turn, they seem intent on hitting you. You shout for them to look out, but they don't.

Then your canoe is hit hard. Anger bursts open inside you. You scream at whoever is paddling the other canoe, leaning in their direction to make your point more strongly.

It is only then that you realize the other canoe is empty. Wind and current, not malicious intent, drove the other canoe into yours. What happens to your anger?

If you're like most people, your anger disappears. But it doesn't gradually fade away or slowly dissipate. As soon as you know the truth, your anger vanishes.[24*] In fact, laughter may replace it, as well as a sense of relief. You may even feel a bit foolish.

Forgiveness happens when you realize that the canoe is empty. Knowing this frees you from anger and allows you to move on.

[24*] This is called *rajja-sarpa* (snake-rope) in Vedanta and refers to one who mistakes a rope for a snake. Reacting to the delusion of the snake you are trapped in fear. As soon as the delusion is replaced by the reality of the rope your fear vanishes effortlessly. All that is required of you is to see what is (*tathata, koach mah*) rather than what you imagine must be.

CLEANSING

The final quality is *nakay*, cleansing. What needs cleansing is our view of the world.

> We human beings are part of the whole called by us Universe, a part limited in time and space. We experience ourselves, our thoughts, and feelings as something separated from the rest, a kind of optical delusion of our consciousness. This delusion is a kind of prison for us, restricting us to our personal desires and to affection for a few persons nearest to us. Our task must be to free ourselves from this prison by widening our circle of compassion to embrace all living creatures and the whole of nature in its beauty.[25]

Nakay is the cleansing of this delusion of separateness: freeing ourselves from the delusion of being apart. and knowing that we—you, I, and all of us—are aspects of the Whole we call YHVH/Tao/Sunyata. Thus, nakay brings us back full circle to the first two Thirteen Qualities: knowing God as Self and Other.

You are a perfect image of Ehyeh/ YHVH/Tao/Sunyata, the One True Reality. You already have the innate capacity for creativity, compassion, grace, equanimity, utmost kindness, truth, forgiveness, and cleansing.

Chances are, however, that when you look in a mirror, you don't see Ehyeh/YHVH/Tao/Sunyata, but an isolated and alienated being struggling with a heap of attractions,

---

[25] Albert Einstein in a condolence letter to Rabbi Robert S. Marcus on the death of his son due to polio. The letter was written in 1950 and quoted in the *New York Times*, March 29, 1972.

distractions, contradictions, repulsions, passions, and conflicts. The cleansing that is nakay is not a matter of changing from one state into another, but of realizing that all states are part of God's manifest reality. If you know all is Ehyeh/YHVH/Tao/Sunyata, then you know that your attractions, distractions, contradictions, repulsions, passions, and conflicts are *also* of Ehyeh/YHVH/Tao/Sunyata. And when you know this, you no longer struggle to be anything other than you are. You simply and effortlessly become all that you already are: creative, compassionate, grace-filled, calm, kind, truthful, forgiving, and cleansed of delusion.

• CHAPTER 5 •

THE YOGA OF CONVERSATION

Shimon ben Gamliel used to say, "I was raised on the talk of sages, and yet I find nothing truer than silence."[1] The silence about which Shimon ben Gamliel speaks is what Katagiri Roshi calls "real silence":

> [R]eal silence occurs when we have been driven into a corner and simply cannot move an inch. This seems like a situation of complete despair, but this silence is quite different from despair, because in the arena of despair, the conscious flame of human desire is still burning. But real silence is the state of human existence that passes through this despair. How can we experience this silence? Without everyday life, it is impossible to experience silence.[2]

Everyday life is the field in which "real silence" happens. But it only happens when you engage everyday life without a

[1] *Pirke Avot*, 1:17.
[2] Dainin Katagiri, *Returning to Silence: Zen Practice in Daily Life* (Shambhala Publications, 1988), 1.

script, without premeditation, without the intermediaries of isms and ideologies: in other words, when you engage everyday life from the perspective of *mochin d'gadlut*, spacious mind. To paraphrase the teaching of Martin Buber, the essential quality of this perspective is not to see things apart from God, or to no longer see things at all but to see God alone, but rather to see things as unique expressions of God. As the advaita/nondual Vedanta teacher Adi Shankaracharya (700-750) taught, "The world is *maya*. Only Brahman is real. Brahman is the world."

The world is maya, illusory, when we imagine the parts are as they appear to narrow mind: independent autonomous selves. When we see through the illusion and see reality from the perspective of spacious mind, we see that the parts are not apart from Brahman, what I am calling Ehyeh/YHVH/Tao/Sunyata, but rather manifestings of Brahman. From this perpective we can engage with and have deep respect for the diverse beings of the world while at the same time knowing they are interdependent expressions of the Be/ing itself. According to Buber, this happens only when all our relations become unbounded for then they become "one relation."[3]

When you engage everyday life from the lesser bounded perspective of *mochin d'katnut*, narrow mind, your relations are bounded by "us" and "them," and you see yourself as separate from and other than the world around you, but when you engage everyday life from *mochin d'gadlut*, spacious mind, you see yourself as an expression of the world within and around you and manifest what Katagiri Roshi calls your "whole personality."

> Whole personality means our individual personality is manifested with the whole universe. All other beings are contents of our personality. So when

---

[3] Martin Buber, *Between Man and Man* (Routledge & Kegan Paul, 1947), 63.

> we manifest our whole personality it is not just our individual personality, but simultaneously through this personality we can feel the whole universe. That is why we can feel magnanimity, tolerance and compassion.[4]

When you engage the world with your "whole personality" you experience "real silence" because you engage each moment without knowing in advance what you are to say and do. In the context of Zen mondo, the exchange of questions and answers between a student and teacher, and *shaylah/shuvah*, question and response between students and rabbis, the "whole personality" emerges when two people are present to one another without the mask and pretense of narrow mind in a relationship where each sees the other as a manifesting of Ehyeh/YHVH/Tao/Sunyata. This is a place of unscripted dialogue. The silence is not necessarily wordless; it may well be one of unpremeditated speech. It is Lin-Chi's *Kwatz!* which silences the monks and Rabbi Joshua's *Lo ba-shamayyim he!* (It is not in heaven!) that silences God:

> The sages are arguing over the fitness of a baker's oven. All but Rabbi Eliezer agree that the oven is unfit for human use. Failing to convince his colleagues with rational arguments, Eliezer turns to the supernatural: "Let this carob tree prove my case!" he says pointing to a tree in the courtyard. The carob tree uproots itself and replants itself one hundred cubits away. "A carob tree proves nothing," the rabbis say. "Then let this stream prove my case," and the stream running beside the study hall begins

---

[4] Katagiri, *Returning to Silence*, 7.

flowing backward. Again the rabbis object, "What does a stream know of such matters?" "Then let the stonewalls of this study hall make my case," and the walls begin to collapse in upon the sages. Rabbi Joshua rebuked the stones which refused to fall out of respect for Joshua but refused to right themselves out of respect for Eliezer. Frustrated, Rabbi Eliezer calls upon God to witness to the rightness of his position. A heavenly Voice addresses the sages, "Why are you arguing with Rabbi Eliezer? His position is correct in every respect!" Rabbi Joshua leaps to his feet and shouts skyward quoting Torah, "*Lo ba-shamayyim he!* It is not in heaven!" (Deuteronomy 30:12). You have given us the means to determine what is true and what is false. It is not for You to interfer in our discussions." Sometime later the Prophet Elijah who was with God during this event was asked how God responded to Joshua's rebuke. "The Holy One laughed joyously saying, 'At last, at last, My children have defeated Me, My children have defeated Me!'"[5]

Rabbi Joshua's *Lo ba-shamayyim he!* was a spontaneous expression of his whole personality, an example of real silence that silenced even God. This kind of dialogue is what Jeremy Engels calls the yoga of conversation:

> All sincere conversation is the worship of the divinity in other people…In all conversation between two persons, tacit reference is made, as to a third

---

[5] Talmud, Baba Metzia 59b.

party, to a common nature. That third part or common nature is not social; it is impersonal; it is God.[6]

With the sole exception of the first dialogue, all the dialogues recalled in this chapter are between me and the students who attended my seminars and retreats. They were spontaneous and unscripted. The point of each of these exchanges wasn't to answer questions, but to respond to questioners. In them, I wasn't relaying information, but offering living words. Anything less would be a scripted idolatry and dead on arrival. The first dialogue occurred between me and my mechanic as I picked up my car at his shop.

ONE THING

Mechanic: I'm a devoted follower of Christ, and I really want to know but I don't want to be rude, but is it OK if I ask you what is the one real difference between Jews and Christians?

Rabbi Rami: Sure. Jews believe that every human—I would say every being—is a direct expression of God, and that no one needs an intermediary to get in touch with God. Christians believe that an intermediary is necessary, and Jesus Christ is that intermediary.

Mechanic: So you don't believe in Jesus?

RR: It isn't a matter of belief. For Jews, Jesus is unnecessary. Whereas for you he is essential. You believe that "No one comes to God except through Jesus."[7] We Jews say along with our cousin Jesus, "I and God are one."[8]

---

[6] Jeremy David Engels. *The Ethics of Oneness: Emerson, Whitman, and the Bhagavad Gita* (University of Chicago Press, 2021), 49-50.
[7] John 14:6.
[8] John 10:30.

Mechanic: That is beautiful, brother. (And then he hugged me.)

A SINGLE STEP

Questioner: Do you believe that every journey begins with a single step?

Rabbi Rami: Sure, and every journey ends the same way. So, tell me, when you take your next step, are you leaving or arriving?

FEAR OF THE UNKNOWN

Q: What keeps me stuck is my fear of the unknown. How do I overcome this fear?

RR: Nobody fears the unknown. What you fear is the known you project onto the unknown. Pretending that what keeps you stuck is the unknown allows you to remain stuck without having to take responsibility for being stuck. Stuck or unstuck, just be honest with yourself.

THERE IS NO "I"

Q: What do you make of the fact that there is no "I" in "team"?

RR: Nothing. What do you make of the fact that there is no "I" in "me"?

THOU ART THAT

Q: I was a born a Jew, but I find Hinduism truer. Especially the notion of *Tat tvam asi,*

You are That, you are Brahman, the Absolute Reality.[9] I wish Judaism knew that.

RR: Then I will fulfill your wish: read Jeremiah 14:22, *Atah hu YHVH Eloheinu*: You are God, the Infinite Happening happening as all happening.

PERFECT AS I AM

Q: I believe I am perfect just as I am.

RR: That's why you never improve.

AFRAID TO CHANGE

Q: How do I stop being afraid to change?

RR: Don't change. Then there is nothing to fear, and you will stop being afraid. Of course, when you stop being afraid, you will have changed.

ELEGANT EQUATIONS

Q: I'm always looking for elegant equations that speak to the great truths of life. Something like Einstein's $E = mc^2$. Can you offer me something like that in the spiritual world?

RR: Try this: Atman + X = Brahman. Now solve for "X."

WHAT RELIGION WOULD YOU CHOOSE?

Q: If you weren't a Jew, would you choose to be a Buddhist?

RR: I'm a Jew because my parents told me I was a Jew. If my parents told me I was a Buddhist, I'd be a Buddhist. Before

[9] Chandogya Upanishad 6.8.7.

my parents told me any of this, I was God. I still am. Just like you. Being Jewish or Buddhist is their error, not mine.

SELF OR NO SELF

Q: Hinduism says we have a Self, or *Atman*. Buddhism teaches *Anatman*, that there is no Self. What is your take on this?

RR: I think you should investigate for yourself to see whether you have a Self or not. And along the way, periodically ask yourself: who is investigating whom?

BECOMING A MONK

Q: I'm thinking about becoming a Buddhist monk. What do you think?

RR: I'm thinking about becoming a giraffe. Thinking about things is fun. What matters is what you do. There is not much I can do with my thinking about becoming a giraffe. But there is much you can do with your thinking about becoming a Buddhist monk—most notably, become a Buddhist monk. If you're asking me what I think about the idea of you becoming a Buddhist monk, I have no thoughts about this. Become a Buddhist monk and then let me know what you think about being a Buddhist monk; I'm curious to know.

NO THOUGHT

Q: Have you ever experienced the ending of thought?

RR: There is no "me" without thought. If thought ceases, so does "Rami." If "Rami" ceases, there is no experience. I no longer yearn for the ending of thought, which is itself a thought. Thinking and not thinking are the activity of the nondual Aliveness that happens as you and me and everything else. Aliveness does what it does because it cannot do otherwise. That is enough to think about for one day.

WHY CARE?

Q: If everything is this nondual infinite Aliveness, why should I care about the welfare of anyone or anything at all?

RR: As soon as you ask why you should care, you are looking to excuse the fact that you don't care. If I need a reason to care about the welfare of starving children, I am admitting that my starting position is that I don't care about the welfare of starving children.

My guess is, however, that you do care, and your care arises for no reason at all. You see a starving child or a lost child or an abused animal, and your heart opens, and you simply care and feel called to help. This is your true foundation, arising out of the nonduality of all life in the greater Aliveness that is Ehyeh/ YHVH/Tao/Sunyata.

What screws this up is when you are taught that this child belongs to a tribe or a race or a religion that doesn't deserve your care; or that this animal, or that animal, or all animals, are beneath you and undeserving of your care.

You must be taught not to care. But caring breaks through, so you must be taught not to care repeatedly. Don't ask why you should care. Notice that you already care and act on that care. Or, if you look and discover you do not care, look to see what you have been taught that has poisoned your sense of reality and prevented you from caring.

ONE WITH GOD

Q: How do I become one with God?

RR: Asking how you become one with God is like a wave

asking how it can become one with the ocean waving it. It cannot become one because it cannot become two. What is true of the wave is true of you. You cannot become one with God because you cannot be other than God.

IS IT OKAY TO GRIEVE?

Q: I get that each life is the happening of nondual Aliveness. But my mother died recently, and I miss her terribly. I cry over my loss nightly. Is it okay for me to grieve for her?

RR: You aren't choosing to grieve; you just grieve. The grief arises of its own accord. The tears flow of their own accord. You aren't doing these things; they are simply and rightly happening because the conditions for them to happen are such that they must happen. Of course it's okay. What isn't okay is thinking that your grief somehow discounts your understanding of Aliveness.

ARE YOU AFRAID OF DEATH?

Q: I'm scared to death of death (laughter). Are you afraid to die?

RR: I'm afraid of dying, I'm not afraid of death. Dying can be painful, and I'm afraid of pain. I know that I'm supposed to observe my pain and not identify with it, but I've tried this, and I suck at it. I have a very low pain threshold. I promise you that I will take any medicine available to me to dull the pain of my dying. Death, however, is something else.

Not too long ago I was standing in my bathroom shortly before dawn, brushing my teeth and chanting a Hebrew *mantrum: ein od milvado*, "there is nothing but God."[10] Then I wasn't.

---

[10] Deuteronomy 4:35.

Rami was gone. I didn't know this at the time because all sense of "me" was gone and with it all sense of time as well. Psychologically, Rami was dead.

Then Rami returned. Time returned. I returned and found myself crumpled on the bathroom floor. I was back. No memory of what happened, no near-death experience. I was "on," then I was "off," and then I was "on" again. There was no fear because there was no "I" to feel fear (or anything else).

After three days in the cardiac unit at St. Thomas Hospital, I returned home with no explanation of what happened. I had only a memory that it happened and the assurance of half a dozen doctors that it might or might not happen again. And if I did go from "on" to "off," there was no guarantee that I'd come back "on" again.

Scary? Not at all. Why? Because there was no pain in "off."

I'm afraid of dying, which is part of being "on." All my fears are linked to being "on." I am fearless—and I-less—when "off." When there comes a time when you are "off," you will be fearless and I-less, too.

HOW DO I LEARN ABOUT ZEN?

Q: If I were to get one book on Zen, which book would you recommend?

RR: Don't buy a book; buy a cushion. Sit on it. See what happens.

DOES GOD KNOW ME?

Q: Does God know me?

RR: Does an ocean know its waves? No. An ocean *is* its waves; an ocean is its waving. God doesn't know you; God is you.

WHAT IS THE DIFFERENCE BETWEEN ME AND A ROCK?

Q: If everything is a happening of Aliveness, what is the difference between me and a rock?

RR: A rock is incapable of asking such a question.

GOD'S WILL

Q: I grew up praying, "God's will be done on earth as it is in heaven." Is this an empty prayer?

RR: It's not a prayer at all. "God's will be done on earth as it is in heaven" is not a prayer, but an affirmation of what is. This comes from Matthew 6:10, where Jesus instructs his disciples on how to pray. While the following verses are indeed prayers of entreaty—give us our daily bread, forgive our debts, lead us not into temptation, and the like—the opening verse is a statement of fact: God's will *is* done here on earth and throughout the cosmos.

Remember, Jesus was a Jew. For Jesus, God is YHVH, the Happening happening as all happening. The will of God is the way things are at any given moment, and the way things are at any given moment is the way things must be at that moment. This is why the opening verse to Jesus' "prayer" is in fact an affirmation.

TASTE AND SEE

Q: I'm a Catholic, and the one thing that keeps me Catholic is the Eucharist. I get to taste the Body and Blood of Jesus Christ. This is a mystery, yet so concrete! How do you not yearn for something as intimate as this?

RR: I understand the intimacy of the Eucharist completely, but not the mystery. The mystery is an invention of the Church, for the benefit of the clergy, who have a monopoly on the mystery. If you know YHVH as the Happening happening as all happening, then everything you eat is the Body of God and everything you drink is the Blood of God, and everyone and everything you meet is a happening of God. This is why the Psalmist says, "taste and see God."[11] There is nothing more intimate than God. But mystery? Not at all.

CHANGE

Q: Buddhists say that everything is impermanent—everything is in a state of flux. Yet your God says, "I am God; I do not change."[12] Doesn't that make Judaism the opposite of Buddhism?

RR: The noun "God" is static, and as such does suggest that God is the opposite of impermanence. But God's Name isn't the noun "God," but the verb YHVH. Verbs are never static. YHVH is the unending flow of reality, the Happening happening as all happening. The author of Ecclesiastes tells us that reality is *hakol havel*, entirely impermanent, as empty as breath.[13]

When the prophet Malachi hears YHVH say, "I am YHVH, I do not change," we should understand YHVH to be saying, "I am YHVH. I do not change because I *am* change."

PEACE

Q: All I want from my spiritual practice is peace. Is this a worthy goal?

RR: There is a wonderful verse in Isaiah that applies here.

[11] Psalm 34:8.
[12] Malachi 3:6.
[13] Ecclesiastes 1:2.

"Peace, peace to the one who is far and the one who is near."[14] The "one who is far" experiences God as transcendent. The "one who is near" experiences God as immanent. Both seekers, having found God, will find peace, but not the same peace.

The peace of the first is experienced as awe; the peace of the second is experienced as love. A complete peace—*shalom*, from the root *sh-l-m*, wholeness—comes only to those who experience the nondual Divine that embraces both far and near. Their peace is the blending of awe and love. If this is the peace you experience, your peace is worthy of the word "spiritual."

IS SPIRITUALITY SELFISH?

Q: Is my pursuit of enlightenment selfish?

RR: Each morning in the zendo, I would recite the vow, "Sentient beings are innumerable, yet I vow to save them all." Today. as part of my meditation practice, I devote myself to being "a blessing to all the families of the earth."[15] The goal of both statements is the same, and achieving them depends on the realization that all selves are expressions of the One Self, the nondual Aliveness we call YHVH, Tao, Brahman, Mother, Dharmakaya, God, etc. Even if you begin your practice from a sense of self and self-actualization, if you persist, you will drop both in favor of Self and Self-Realization.

[14] Isaiah 57:19.
[15] Genesis 12:3.

PART TWO

HOW TO

[The following chapters are based on talks I have given in various retreat settings. While edited for print, I have done my best to maintain their original informality. Most of these talks were inspired by Zen Master Thich Nhat Hanh's series of short *How To* booklets. I am grateful to Thay for his teaching, the brevity of his words, and his focus on doing.]

• CHAPTER 6 •

HOW TO LISTEN

Long before hatred dominated the City of Peace, I used to visit the Dome of the Rock, the iconic gold-domed Islamic shrine at the center of Al-Aqsa Mosque complex on the Temple Mount in the Old City of Jerusalem. In Hebrew, the "rock" for which the Dome is named, is called *Even Hashtiyya*/The Foundation Stone; in Arabic it is called *al-Sakrah al-Musharrafah*/The Noble Stone. For Jews, this is the cornerstone of creation; for Muslims, this is the rock from which Muhammad ascended to heaven on his Night Journey. The rock is also called the Pierced Stone because there is a stairway carved into it that leads down to a small cave called the Well of Souls, which has been used for prayer by both Christian Crusaders and Muslims.

I would often sit with an old Sufi who spent his days meditating in the Well of Souls. My Arabic was primitive, and we rarely spoke. Mostly he simply smiled and pointed upward through the hole in the Well, inviting me to lose myself in the magnificence of the dome.

During one visit, however, I told him, in hurried English, of an experience I had a few days earlier in the Sinai Desert: I had separated myself from my traveling companions and walked off to meditate. As I sat cross-legged on the sand, eyes closed, silently repeating my mantra—*ein od milvado/*there is nothing but God—I was immersed in and eventually erased by a sound that arose from everywhere and nowhere at the same time.

As I tried to communicate with the old Sufi, he just gazed at me, smiling. I'm sure he didn't understand a word I was saying. Embarrassed, I stopped speaking, apologized awkwardly in Arabic, and rose to leave. The old man motioned me to sit back down. He then started humming. After a few moments of humming, he made a gesture I took to mean, "Did you hear something like that?"

"Yes!" I said in English. "That's it! That's what I heard! What is that?"

The old Sufi smiled widely and in heavily Arabic-accented English replied, "Allah singing the universe alive."

The universe is Allah/Ehyeh/YHVH/Tao/Sunyata. And the universe sings. Or hums. Or vibrates. Genesis calls this "the breath of God *m'rakhefet/*ululating over the deep."[1] 1 Kings calls it *"kol d'mamah daka,* the sheer sound of silence."[2] The ancient rabbis referred to it as *Bat Kol,* the Daughter's Voice.[3] This is the sound Jews are called to hear when we are called to hear the nonduality of YHVH in the Sh'ma: Hear O'Israel.[4] This is the Word that John tells us exists from the beginning.[5] In Sanskrit this sound is called *Nada* and *Omkara,* a never-ending white noise pervading the universe, out of which the primal sound OM arises.

[1] Genesis 1:2.
[2] 1 Kings 19:10.
[3] Talmud, *Bava Metzia* 59b.
[4] Deuteronomy 6:4.
[5] John 1:1.

> [The sound] is a cosmic hum, a scintillating almost electric background sound. Even though it's going on all the time we don't generally notice it.... [But it] is not a thing you have to find—rather you just open to it: it's the ability to listen with your mind in a receptive state, which makes it possible to hear the sound of silence.... Listening to the sound of silence, you can begin to contemplate non-thinking, because when you are just listening to the cosmic sound there is no thought. It's like this—emptiness, not-self. When you're just with the cosmic sound alone, there is pure attention, no sense of a person or personality, of me and mine.[6]

According to the Venerable Chinese Zen Master Hsuan Hua, "the nature of hearing is not subject to coming into being and ceasing to be. Therefore, turn the attention of your hearing-faculty inward...Reverse the direction of your hearing-faculty and listen to your true nature until your nature merges with the unsurpassed path to enlightenment. What is your true nature? When you hear it, you will recognize it."[7]

Listening to the sheer sound of silence awakens you to the transient nature of all happening. Listening to the sheer sound of silence allows you to engage with life without being trapped by your ideas about life. You are free to deal with the actuality of what is happening—good, bad, or indifferent—without being ensnared by what you imagine is or should be happening.

As the Buddhist teacher Ajahn Amaro says, listening to Nada "leads to a knowing awareness with which we can more

---

[6] Ajahn Sumedo, *The Sound of Silence* (Wisdom Publications, 2007), 161, 164.
[7] *The Surangama Sutra with Excerpts from the Commentary by the Venerable Master Hsuan Hua* (Buddhist Text Translation Society, 2009), 257.

easily recognize the transparency, emptiness and insubstantiality of these experiences and let them go."[8]

Listening to the sheer sound of silence is listening to Ehyeh/YHVH/Tao/Sunyata. Doing so frees you from the drama of self and reveals the whole cosmos as one happening, One Word.

> How do you listen? Use your ears. But don't listen to the sounds outside. Don't try to figure out what is happening in the street or who is saying what nearby. Turn the hearing inward and listen inside yourself. In this way your own nature will be revealed. When you have turned your hearing around, you will be set free from external sounds. It is the easiest practice for success in spiritual cultivation.[9]

The practice is deceptively simple: just listen.

> When you employ this *Nada* [sound of silence] as the main support for your meditation, you must follow all its slender fluctuating, subtle variation of note, and mysterious jewel–like glitterings, second by second, with the utmost diligence…. The special benefit you will derive from this mystical sound is priceless. First, it will sustain you in your meditation by giving your attention something definite to hold on to and so allow you to concentrate better with little or no wavering. Second, it will have a particularly purifying and calming effect on your mind as on your feelings. Third, it will help you, little by little, to rise to the higher and more luminous planes of your

[8] www.lionsroar.com/the-sound-of-silence.
[9] *The Surangama Sutra with Excerpts from the Commentary by the Venerable Master Hsuan Hua.* Burlingame, 258.

consciousness. Finally, it will become the means for an ardent and sincere aspirant to become immediately aware when your attention beings to weaken and waver during your meditation…for you will not fail to observe that, at such moments, the sound has either altogether disappeared or has lost its supernal luster and subtle ultravibrations, becoming very distant and pale.[10]

As the sheer sound of silence becomes your primary focus, all other concerns fade into the background. You experience a sense of freedom and calm. It is from this place of tranquility that you can observe the ten thousand joys and ten thousand sorrows of life—or, as the prophet Elijah experienced them, the tornados, earthquakes, and infernos of everyday living.[11] You can watch these events and engage with them without becoming caught in them. You can enter the drama of life to alleviate suffering without adding to the drama or the suffering.

The One Word of Zen Mind/Jewish Mind is ineffable but not inaudible. When you learn to listen to it you will perceive "the Unity of all things—That which is pervading you and everything else at the same time."[12]

---

[10] Edward Salim Michael. *The Law of Attention: Nada Yoga and the Way of Inner Vigilance* (Inner Traditions, 2010), 43 (adapted for inclusive language).

[11] The phrase "sheer sound of silence" comes from 1 Kings 19:10 where the Prophet Elijah's experience this sound after experiencing a series of tornados, earthquakes, and infernos.

[12] Salim Michael. *The Law of Attention*, 61 (adapted for inclusive language).

• CHAPTER 7 •

HOW TO SPEAK

The Hasidim tell a story about a man who loved to gossip. As he grew into old age, he realized the harm his speech had caused, and he sought his rabbi's advice on how to make amends and be forgiven.

The rabbi instructed the man to go to the marketplace, purchase two of the finest feather pillows he could find, take them to the hilltop overlooking the village, tear them open, and spill the feathers into the wind.

Thinking repentance would be much harder to achieve than this, the man happily ran to the marketplace, purchased his pillows, tossed the feathers into the wind, and watched with satisfaction as they were blown throughout the village. He returned to the rabbi and awaited forgiveness.

"Not just yet," the rabbi told him. There was one more thing to do. He had to walk through the village, retrieve the feathers, and repack the pillows.

"But that's impossible," the man said. "Those feathers have gone everywhere; there's no way I can take them back now."

The rabbi nodded solemnly and said, "What is true of

feathers is true of words. Once spoken, they can never be retrieved. The harm caused by gossip cannot be undone."

In Hebrew, working with speech is called *Shmirat HaLashon*: guarding your tongue against damaging or derogatory remarks that can cause a person physical, psychological, financial, or spiritual harm. This is what Buddhists call Right Speech. In the *Abhaya Raja-kumara Sutta*, the Buddha says this about Right Speech:

> Regarding words that the Wise know to be misleading, false, unhelpful, divisive and disagreeable to others, they do not say them.

> Regarding words that the Wise know to be accurate and honest yet unhelpful, divisive and disagreeable to others, they do not say them.

> Regarding words that the Wise know to be accurate, honest, and helpful, but divisive and disagreeable to others, they are careful to say them only at the proper time and in the proper place.

> Regarding words that the Wise know to be misleading, false, and unhelpful, but endearing and agreeable to others, they do not say them.

> Regarding words that the Wise know to be accurate and honest, yet unhelpful, even if they are endearing and agreeable to others, they do not say them.

> Regarding words that the Wise know to be accurate, honest, helpful, endearing and agreeable to others,

they are careful to say them only at the proper time and in the proper place.

Why is this? Because the Wise have sympathy for all living beings.[1]

Millennia later, Rabbi Meir ha-Kohen Kagan (1838-1933), called the Chofetz Chaim (Seeker of Life) after the title of his book on proper speech, provided his own guidelines for right speech:

Do not spread a negative image of someone, even if that image is true.

Do not share information that can cause physical, financial, emotional, or spiritual harm.

Do not embarrass people, even in jest.

Do not pretend that writing or body language or innuendo is not speech.

Do not speak against a community, race, ethnic group, gender, or age group.

Do not gossip, even with those closest to you.

Do not repeat gossip, even when what you say is generally known.

---

[1] *Abhaya Sutta*, Majjhima Nikaya 58, my rendition.

> Do not tell people negative things said about them,
> for this can lead to needless conflict.
>
> Do not listen to gossip. Give everyone the benefit of
> the doubt.[2]

If you are looking for something simpler, try this rule of thumb from a teaching of the Baal Shem Tov: Every human being is born with a fixed number of words to speak. What words you speak is up to you; how many you may speak before you die is determined at your birth. When you have spoken the last of your allotted number of words you die. Since you never know how many words you have left, before you say anything at all ask yourself this: "Is the word I am about to utter, a word I am willing to die for?"

---

[2] Yisrael Meir Kagan, Sefer Chafetz Chayim, *Chofetz Chayim* (Brooklyn: Mazal Press, 2008).

• CHAPTER 8 •

HOW TO SEE

A Tibetan Buddhist friend and I were walking a gentle trail in Aspen, Colorado. After a few minutes, he stopped and drew my attention to the tops of the surrounding mountains. He pulled a book out from a cloth bag he had slung over his shoulder. "Just rest your eyes on the mountain tops while I read something to you," he said.

> By contemplating the openness of space, the only nonphysical element, we can experience the openness of our own nature. Space is emptiness and immateriality. Space provides room for everything else, including the other physical elements.
>
> Look out at the deep blue sky and feel its immaterial, nongrasping nature. See and feel its vastness and limitless quality—the infinity of sky. Be aware, in your mortal body, of space and openness beyond questions or elaborations, beyond time or place. Let go of your thoughts and worries, and be at one with the nature of sky. We can feel great peace looking at the sky, especially from a place with a broad view

on a clear day. But any glimpse of the sky can grant us peace. Gazing at the night sky, especially when it is clear, will also encourage a meditative state of mind.

The boundless sky has more than enough room for our suffering. Practice releasing into space all your pain, stresses, and grasping. Imagine that all worries and negative thoughts disappear there, like mist or clouds that disperse with a trace. Appreciate any feeling of comfort or peace that comes to you.[1]

"What do you think?" he asked. But I wasn't thinking. I couldn't say a word. I was lost in the vastness that was This.

It was this practice of sky-gazing that opened me to the deeper meaning of a Jewish teaching I had chanted most of my life: *Esa einai el heharim, may'eyin yavo ezri. Ezri me'im YHVH, oseh shamayim va'aretz*: "I lift up my eyes to the mountains, *may'eyin* does my help come? My help comes from YHVH happening as all happening throughout the cosmos."

I deliberately left the Hebrew word *may'eyin* untranslated. The conventional rendering of may'eyin is "from where:" "from where does my help come?" May'eyin, however, can also be read as *may*/from *eyin*/no-thingness where *eyin* is another word for the ineffable YHVH, the Happening happening as all happening. Read this way, may'eyin isn't a question—"from where?"— but an affirmation: from *Eyin*, from YHVH: *My help comes from the vast Emptiness manifesting the cosmos* (literally earth and heavens).

Once this understanding of *Esa Einai* is grasped intellectually, it can be experienced directly when you turn Esa Einai into a practice: the Jewish version of Tibetan sky-gazing.

[1] Tulku Thondrup, *The Healing Power of Mind* (Shambhala Publications, 1996), 143.

Here is my Jewish sky-gazing practice, adapted from the teaching of my friend Lama Surya Das:

> Go outdoors and sit comfortably. Eyes closed. Inhale and exhale naturally. Relax. When you are ready, open your eyes and gaze softly at the horizon.
>
> As you gaze into the horizon silently and slowly recite the *Esa Einai*: *Esa einai el heharim, may'eyin yavo ezri. Ezri me'im YHVH, oseh shamayim va'aretz* / As I gaze toward the horizon, I see the No-thing happening as everything, and in this seeing is my comfort and support.
>
> Repeat the *Esa Einai* until doing so seems unnecessary. Then just gaze.
>
> Allow the breath to merge you with the vastness of space. Allow the breath to unfurl spacious mind.
>
> If thoughts arise, watch as they flow out into space. If feelings arise, watch as they flow out into space. If sensations arise, watch as they flow out into space.
>
> Just rest in the infinity that is the Name beyond speaking, the Tao beyond naming.
>
> When you wish to return, shift your gaze from sky to earth. Notice the world around you.
>
> Softly say, "May I and all beings be free. May I and all beings be peaceful. May I and all beings be kind. May I and all beings be just."[2]

A companion practice to Esa Einai is *Shiviti*, "I Place." Where the former is a more formal meditative practice, the

---

[2] Lama Surya Das, *Awakening the Buddha Within* (Broadway Books, 1997), 363-64.

latter is done amid your everyday encounters. *Shiviti* comes from Psalm 16:8: *Shiviti YHVH l'negdi tamid*: "I place the Divine before me always."

Since the Name of God, YHVH, is unpronounceable, the ancient rabbis offered euphemisms to say in its place. The one I use here is *Shekhinah*, a feminine-gendered word meaning "the Presence of God." I recite the verse this way: *Shiviti Shekhinah l'negdi tamid*.

Unlike in Esa Einai where you rest your gaze on the horizon, with Shiviti practice you rest your gaze on another being reminding yourself that who you are seeing is a manifesting of YHVH by silently reciting *Shiviti Shekhinah l'negdi tamid*. Seeing this way calls you to treat all beings with kindness and respect.

The French Jewish philosopher Emmanuel Levinas taught what is called an *ethic of the face*: when you see the face of another being, human or otherwise, you feel inwardly commanded to treat that being with justice, compassion, and love. This is so because seeing the face of another is seeing the Face of God, the Face of YHVH, or what Zen Master Daito Kokushi called your "original face which was before father or mother was born...the state before heaven and earth were parted, before you received human form. The original face is really nameless, but it is indicated by such terms as...Buddha nature."[3]

When I teach Shiviti there is often the complaint that Torah explicitly says we cannot see the Face of God and live.[4] While this is true, we also told to seek God's Face.[5] How can we do both? My understanding is simple: when we see God's Face as every face we can no longer live as we did before we saw God's Face as every face. Seeing the face of the other as the other is seeing the other through the lens of narrow mind. Seeing the

---

[3] Trevor Leggett, *A First Zen Reader* (Tuttle, 1974), 21.
[4] Exodus 33:20.
[5] Psalm 27:8.

face of the other as the Face of God is seeing the other through the lens of spacious mind. Moving from narrow mind to spacious mind is the gift that comes with the practice of Shiviti.

• CHAPTER 9 •

HOW TO EAT

In Thich Nhat Hanh's delightful little book *How to Eat*, he focuses on the mindfulness of eating:

> When you put a piece of fruit in your mouth, all you need is a little bit of mindfulness to be aware: "I am putting a piece of apple in my mouth." Your mind doesn't need to be somewhere else....Then you can look more deeply and in just a very short time you will see the apple seed, the beautiful orchard and the sky, the farmer, the picker, and so on. A lot of work is in that apple![1]

And perhaps a lot of exploitation as well. How well was the earth treated in the growing of that apple? How well was the farmer treated? How well was the apple picker treated? What is the cost to the planet of shipping apples around the globe so that people who wish to eat apples mindfully can do so in the off-season, or in places where apples do not grow naturally?

[1] Thich Nhat Hanh, *How to Eat* (Parallax Press, 2014), 8-9.

Thay's concern is with inter-being: the interdependence and co-arising of all things in the greater unified reality in which they live, and change, and exist. Turning our attention to a slice of bread, he reminds us that this bread "has not come from nothing."

> Bread comes from wheat fields, from hard work, and from the baker, the supplier, and the seller. But the bread is more than that. The wheat field needs clouds and sunshine. So in this slice of bread there is sunshine, there is cloud, there is the labor of the farmer, the joy of having flour, and the skill of the baker and then—miraculously!—there is the bread. The whole cosmos has come together so that this piece of bread can be in your hand.[2]

What is true of our bread is true of our bodies as well. We, too, are a result of the cosmos coming together, and eating mindfully is a cosmic celebration of this cosmic creativity.

Thich Nhat Hanh also tells us that when we eat, we need "to pay attention to...the food that we are eating and our friends who are sitting around us and eating with us. This is called mindfulness of food and mindfulness of community."[3] Zen Mind/Jewish Mind goes a bit further paying attention as well to the workers who grow the food and bring it to our table:

> The Buddhist point of view takes the function of work to be at least threefold: to give workers a chance to utilize and develop their faculties; to enable them to overcome their ego-centeredness by

[2] Nhat Hanh, *How to Eat*, 10.
[3] Nhat Hanh, *How to Eat*, 16.

joining with other people in a common task; and to bring forth the goods and services needed...[4]

Because "What's for dinner?" is a profoundly moral question, it is a deeply controversial one as well:

> There are controversies over what we should eat. There are controversies over where our food should come from. There are controversies over how our food should be grown. There are controversies over food technologies. There are controversies over food distribution. There are controversies over food policies.... Food issues and choices are very often ethical issues and choices. They concern rights, justice, power, autonomy, control, sustainability, animal welfare and human well-being.... We cannot make good choices about food consumption, food policy or food systems without attending to food ethics.[5]

Knowing you are a unique expression of nondual Aliveness carries with it the powerful ethical imperative of the Golden Rule.

Confucius was the first to articulate the Golden Rule: "One word which sums up the basis of all good conduct.... loving-kindness. Do not do to others what you do not want done to yourself."[6] However, the Rule appears (in some form) in every major religion:

---

[4] E. F. Schumacher, *Small is Beautiful: Economics as if People Mattered* (Harper & Row, 1989), 58-59, adapted for inclusivity.
[5] Ronald Sandler, *Food Ethics: The Basics* (Routledge, 2015), 1-2.
[6] *Analects* 15:23.

Judaism: That which is hateful to you do not do to another.[7]

Christianity: Do unto others what you would have others do unto you.[8]

Islam: No one of you is a believer until you desire for others that which you desire for yourself.[9]

Hinduism: This is the sum of duty: do not do to others that if done to you would cause you suffering.[10]

Buddhism: Do nothing to others that you yourself would find hurtful.[11]

Jainism: Treat all creatures in the world as you would like to be treated.[12]

Taoism: Regard your neighbor's gain as your gain, your neighbor's loss as your loss.[13]

Zoroastrianism: Do not do to others whatever is injurious to yourself.[14]

Bahá'í: Lay not on any soul a load that you would

---

[7] Talmud, *Shabbat* 31a.
[8] Matthew 7:12.
[9] Muhammad, Hadith.
[10] *Mahabharata* 5, 1517.
[11] *Udana–Varga* 5,1.
[12] *Sutrakritanga* 1.11.33.
[13] *Tai Shang Kan Yin P'ein.*
[14] *Shayast-na-Shayast* 13.29.

not wish to be laid upon you, and desire not for anyone the things you would not desire for yourself.[15]

The Golden Rule doesn't provide a list of specific right and wrong behaviors. In this way, it allows for cultural and ethical diversity. But it does apply a single moral standard to that diversity. If you know that all life is a manifesting of nondual Aliveness, you are committed to alleviating, minimizing, and doing the best you can to not contribute to the suffering of other beings, and your diet becomes an opportunity to express that understanding and commitment, regardless of your culture or ethical background.

From the perspective of Jewish Mind this leads us to wres-tling with the tradition of *kashrut* or kosher. *Kosher* literally means "fit"—i.e., fit for human consumption: "And God said, 'Behold every seed-bearing plant and seed-bearing fruit tree: these I have given you to eat.'"[16] Originally, a kosher diet was a vegan diet, but things changed after Noah's flood:

> God blessed Noah and his children and said to them: "Be fruitful and multiply, and fill the earth. Every animal of the earth, every bird of the sky, everything that creeps upon the ground, and all the fish of the sea shall fear and dread you, for into your hand they are delivered. Every moving thing that lives shall be food for you. Where once I gave you the green plants, now I give you everything."[17]

For me the tale of Noah is a story rather than as history, and I assume the author of the story is using the story to convey

[15] Bahá'u'lláh, *Gleanings*.
[16] Genesis 1:29. The focus on seed bearing trees and plants is to limit consumption to renewable resources.
[17] Genesis 9:1-3.

a moral. While there is logic for allowing humans to consume meat after the flood given that the earth was too wet to plant, the fact that Torah tells us that humanity's abandonment of its original vegan diet led to animals experiencing fear and dread when they were among humans suggests that the author of the story is telling something far more profound: consuming animals disrupts the natural relationship between humans and animals.

One way (but not the only way) to apply the Golden Rule to what you eat and restore the original harmony between humans and animals is to return to the original kosher vegan diet. If humankind were to do this, it would put an end to much of animals' fear and dread of us. It would also reclaim our mission to serve and protect nature, [18] rather than to dominate and exploit her.[19]

You may not decide to become a vegan (or a vegetarian, or, like me, a pescetarian—someone who eats some fish in an otherwise vegetarian diet), but that doesn't preclude you from taking up some form of kashrut.

The primary principle behind kashrut is *tsa'ar ba'alei hayim*, the prevention of cruelty to animals.[20] The prophet Habakkuk makes it clear that human destruction of wildlife will lead to humanity's destruction,[21] and the prophet Jeremiah along with the authors of Proverbs and Job, celebrates the intelligence of animals.[22] The medieval instruction manual *Sefer Hasidim* (*The Book of the Pious*) states, "Be kind and compassionate to all creatures…. Never beat nor inflict pain on any animal, beast, bird, or insect." The *Shulchan Aruch* (*Prepared Table*), the sixteenth-century code of Jewish law, states that "[I]t is forbidden by Jewish law to inflict pain upon any living creature. Indeed, we must

---

[18] Genesis 2:15.

[19] Genesis 1: 26-28.

[20] Talmud, *Bava Metzia* 32b.

[21] Habakkuk 2:17.

[22] Jeremiah 8:7-8; Proverbs 6:6-8, 30:24-28; Job 12:7-10.

relieve the pain of any creature, even if it is ownerless or belongs to one who is not bound by Jewish law."

The Buddhist version of *tsa'ar ba'alei hayim* is well articulated by the twentieth-century economist and philosopher E.F. Schumacher:

> While the materialist is mainly interested in goods, the Buddhist is mainly interested in liberation. But Buddhism is "The Middle Way" and therefore is in no way antagonistic to physical well-being. It is not wealth that stands in the way of liberation but the attachment to wealth; not the enjoyment of pleasurable things but the craving for them. The keynote of Buddhist economics, therefore, is simplicity and non-violence. From an economist's point of view, the marvel of the Buddhist way of life is the utter rationality of its pattern—amazingly small means leading to extraordinarily satisfactory results... [C]onsumption is merely a means to human well-being, the aim should be to obtain the maximum of well-being with the minimum of consumption.[23]

Once Torah allowed for the eating of meat, the rabbis sought to minimize its consumption by inventing *shechitah*, the laws of kosher slaughtering. This must be done by a trained and rabbinically licensed *shochet*/kosher slaughterer. The killing must be done using a blade that is kept sharp and that is inspected after each use, to ensure that it is free of any imperfections that might cause the animal being killed any unnecessary pain. The blade must sever the trachea and the esophagus in a single stroke, without hesitation—and without chopping, tearing, or burrowing between the

---

[23] Schumacher, *Small is Beautiful*, 60.

trachea and the esophagus, or under the skin of the animal, or outside the approved area for the incision. All of this is done to minimize the suffering of the animal. The meat must then be drained of blood, and blood vessels, veins, and certain sinews and fats must be removed as well. In other words, while Torah allows for the eating of meat, the rabbis made procuring kosher meat so difficult as to make eating it quite rare (pun intended).

In addition to minimizing the suffering of animals, ethicist Peter Singer provides us with the following principles for eating with Zen Mind/Jewish Mind:[24]

> *Transparency*: While we might disagree as to what is unnecessary suffering regarding the treatment of animals, we cannot have any authentic conversation about ethical eating if we are kept ignorant of how our food is prepared.

> *True Cost*: We have the right to know the impact food manufacturing has on the environment, and the neighborhood in which a processing plant operates.

> *Social Responsibility*: Workers should be treated fairly and with dignity, paid adequately, provided with safe working conditions, and free from harassment of any kind.

> *Needs*: Our survival is often at the cost of the lives of other beings. This is largely unavoidable. What is avoidable is cheapening the lives of other beings by taking their lives for reasons not tied to our survival but to laziness, convenience, and habit.

---

[24] Peter Singer and Jim Mason, *The Way We Eat: Why Our Food Choices Matter.* New York: Rodale, 2006, pp. 270-271.

· CHAPTER 10 ·

HOW TO PRAY

I haven't prayed in synagogue in years.[1] I find the liturgy too wordy, the service too long, and the need to translate the dualism inherent in the prayers into the nondualism of my experience too exhausting.

Judaism being a communal affair, I'm supposed to confess sadness over this, or at least to grieve the loss of community that synagogue attendance offers. But I feel neither sadness nor loss. When I sit in silent meditation, either alone or with others, I commune with each life in the greater Aliveness that is all life. My absence from synagogue services, however, doesn't mean I don't pray at all. I do. All day long.

The verb "to pray" in Hebrew is *hitpallel*, it means "self-observation." While the liturgy of Jewish prayer is aimed at a god outside yourself, the goal of *hitpallel* is to observe yourself and realize your true nature as Ehyeh/YHVH/Tao/Sunyata.

What a great wonder that we should be able to

---

[1] I do go to synagogue to learn and to teach. It is a synagogue's library rather than its sanctuary that attracts me.

> draw so near to YHVH in prayer. How many walls there are between YHVH and human beings! Even though YHVH fills all the world, YHVH is so very hidden! Yet a single word of prayer can topple all the walls and bring you close to YHVH.[2]

This teaching, from Rabbi Dov Ber of Mezeritch (1704-72), requires some unpacking.

Dov Ber was a nondualist. For him, there were (and are) no actual walls between YHVH and humans—or YHVH and anything else—since there is nothing else but YHVH, "and in truth the whole earth is full of God's glory, and there is no place devoid of God…and in every place there is divinity."[3]

God is "hidden" behind the dead words of religion and the psychological delusions of *mochin d'katnut*, the narrow mind that imagines God as other. When Dov Ber speaks of being "close to YHVH," the word he uses is *devekut*—the realization "that material reality, as a separate realm of existence, is not ultimately real, but rather that its existence is merely apparent, whereas the only true reality is the all-pervasive divine presence."[4] And all it takes to topple the illusion, and awaken us to the nonduality of all life in the greater Aliveness of YHVH, is a single word or phrase.

The recitation of a single word or phrase refers to the practice of *hagah*, what in Sanskrit is called *mantra japa*.[5] *Hagah* finds its sister practice in the Tibetan Buddhist recitation of *Om mani padme hum*, and the Pure Land Buddhist recitation of the *Nembutsu*, the name of Amitabha Buddha, the Buddha of Infinite Light.

---

[2] Dov Ber of Mezeritch, *Likkutim Yekarim*, Korets 1781, fol. 4b.

[3] Dov Ber of Mezeritch, *Likkutei Amarim*, Korets 1781, fol. 26b.

[4] Elior, *The Paradoxical Ascent to God*, 14.

[5] *Mantram* is singular, *mantra* is plural.

> Whoever writes [or recites] *Om Manipadme Hum...*
> is said to have written [or recited] the eighty-four
> thousand dharmas, shorthand for the idea of the
> complete Buddhist literary corpus. The formula is
> also... said to be the means by which 'the twelvefold
> wheel of Dharma is turned,' referring to another
> well-known phrase used to denote the entirety of
> all Buddhist teaching. It is, elsewhere, said to be the
> indestructible instruction on all wisdom.[6]

My experience reciting *Om Manipadme Hum* is limited, but my Buddhism professor Taitetsu Unno was a Pure Land Buddhist priest, and he taught me to recite the *Nembutsu*.

> Ultimate reality in Buddhism is called *dharmakaya*;
> it is beyond description, imagination, and concep-
> tion. Since it transcends the horizon of our under-
> standing, it reveals itself in our world as the Name,
> *namu-amida-butsu*, making itself accessible to anyone
> at any time. To truly hear the Name-that-calls is to
> be led out of darkness into the light of day.[7]

We can of course say the same of YHVH, as well. The reality for which it stands is beyond expression, yet is revealed in the Name itself. Reciting the Name—whether we are talking about *namu-amida-butsu* or one of the *mantra* found in Judaism— "is awakening to the incomparable worth of this unrepeatable life, this limited, finite life that is inseparable from boundless, infinite

---

[6] Alexander Studholme, *The Origins of Om Manipadme Hum: A Study of the Karandavyauha Sutra* (SUNY Press, 2002), 72.
[7] Taitetsu Unno, *River of Fire, River of Water* (Doubleday, 1998), 33.

life."[8] This is because the Name—whether *namu-amida-butsu* or YHVH—is reality itself:

> The saying of *nembutsu* confirms the boundless, endless life (*amida-butsu*) in which the insecure self (*namu*) finds itself at home. Human reason cannot fathom the fullness of living *namu-amida-butsu*, for much of it is beyond our conscious awareness.... Philosophically speaking, the *nembutsu* is the self-articulation of fundamental reality. As such, the saying of the Name contains the alpha and omega of the Buddhist soteriological path.... The Name, *namu-amida-butsu* is the source of creative life, the power that affirms reality-as-is. Each time it is intoned, vital life is experienced. What does this mean? Through the working of the Name, we are made to become aware of ourselves as limited, finite beings (*namu*), yet secure within the sustaining power of boundless compassion (*amida-butsu*). As human beings we are made to become true, real, and sincere through the operative functioning of the Name. When we thus em-*body* the Name, Amida is right here. Apart from intoning the Name, there is no Amida. The Name is Amida Buddha. The Name is reality-as-is.[9]

The Name Amida is reality. The Name YHVH is no less so: "There is nothing that exists other than YHVH, for YHVH animates and vitalizes all beings. YHVH is the reality of all existence, and there is no reality other than YHVH."[10] Chanting

[8] Unno, *River of Fire, River of Water*, 229.
[9] Unno, *River of Fire, River of Water*, 28.
[10] Rabbi Avraham of Slonim, the Slonimer Rebbe (1804-83), *Sefer Netivot Shalom al ha-Torah* 2:161.

either Name awakens you to your true nature as a manifesting of this reality.

The challenge of chanting YHVH, of course, is that the Name itself is literally unpronounceable. Jewish mystics have dealt with this challenge by offering a variety of alternative words or phrases to recite during the practice of hagah. We will come to some of these shortly.

Hagah means "to coo like a dove." Over time hagah erases the delusion that we are apart from, rather than a part of, the greater reality of YHVH. As the Indian-born scholar, author, and meditation teacher Eknath Easwaran writes:

> The mantram is the living symbol of the profoundest reality that the human being can conceive of, the highest power that we can respond to and love. When we repeat the mantram in our mind, we are reminding ourselves of the supreme reality enshrined in our hearts. It is only natural that the more we repeat the mantram, the deeper it will sink into our consciousness. As it goes deeper, it will strengthen our will, heal the old divisions in our consciousness that now cause us conflict and turmoil, and give us access to deeper resources of strength, patience, and love, to work for the benefit of all.[11]

The Hebrew Bible traces the practice of hagah to the time of Seth, the third son of Eve and Adam: "At that time, they began to call upon the name of YHVH."[12] This was the earliest form of prayer, simple and concise: just calling out the Name of

---

[11] Eknath Easwaran, *The Mantram Handbook*. Tomales (Nilgiri Press, 2009), 20.
[12] Genesis 4:26.

God. No specific posture, no priesthood or intermediary: just a human being repeating the Name of God.

It may be the case that in Seth's time, the Name YHVH was pronounceable. If so, that time is long past. Today we substitute other names or phrases for the ineffable YHVH. Among the mantra I recite daily are *HaRachaman*/the Compassionate One, *Ein od milvado*/there is nothing but God, and *Shiviti Shekhinah l'negdi tamid*/I place the Divine before me always.

There is no one correct mantram, only the mantram that speaks to you. As the prophet Micah said, "Each person will walk in the Name of their God.[13]

The key is to discover a mantram that resonates with you. Experiment with different mantra to see which mantram opens your heart and fulfills the teaching of the prophet Joel: "All who call upon God's Name will escape."[14] Escape from what? From the delusion that you are apart from the Whole rather than forever a part of it.

If you are unsure about which mantram to use, I suggest you begin with the one Levi Yitzchak of Berditchev used: *HaRachaman*/the Compassionate One. Levi Yitzchak wrote of his awakening in a poem called "You, Beloved":

> Where can I find You, and where can I not find
> You?
> Above? Only You.
> Below? Only You.
> To the East? Only You.
> To the West? Only You.
> To the South? Only You.
> To the North? Only You.

---

[13] Micah 4:5.
[14] Joel 3:5 in the Hebrew Bible; Joel 2:32 in Christian Bibles.

> If it is good? It is You.
> If it is not? Also You.
> It is You. It is always and only You.

In hagah practice, the mantram is recited in sets of one hundred and one repetitions: "It is good to recite a teaching one hundred times; it is better to recite it one hundred and one times." [15] The rabbis also suggest you experiment with any given mantram for forty days so that "it will be rooted in your memory as if it were placed in your pocket."[16] If this does not happen, you are advised to try another mantram.

Over time, hagah will become second nature to you, and there will be moments when "you will be so absorbed in this practice that all thoughts of self-judging or self-criticism will cease. There will be nothing but the flow of life."[17]

Reb Zalman Schachter–Shalomi taught me that if I were diligent in my hagah practice, there would come a time when the mantram would repeat subconsciously of its own accord and rise into my conscious mind whenever the need arose. Eknath Easwaran says something similar:

> At the most superficial level, repetition of the mantram causes the brain to swing from barely connected thoughts to a simple phrase that holds the attention and thus slows down the mind.... In this way, the mental repetition of a simple phrase like a mantram can provide a guidewire to move your attention away from a troubling stream of thoughts. It is as though the mantram provides access to a peaceful, grounded center that puts our cravings,

---

[15] Talmud, *Chagigah* 9b.
[16] Talmud, *Pesachim* 72a. the rabbis took the word "times" to mean "days."
[17] Dov Baer, *Or Ha-Emet* 2b, my translation.

> drives, and other immediate needs in perspective…. After I had repeated the mantram consciously over a period of time, I found the words arising naturally when I faced a situation of fear or distress. In fact, now I sometimes become aware of the mantram repeating itself before I actually realize that I am in a predicament.[18]

I can attest to the truth of this from my own experience. Whenever I am anxious, worried, annoyed, or angry, if I shift my attention to the recitation of *HaRachaman*—Compassionate One—my breathing slows, my heart rate follows suit, my muscles relax and the insidious tape loop of anger, self-recrimination, and blame playing in my mind quiets down and then shuts off. I am present to the situation and the emotions it triggers, but I am the victim of neither. Anxiety, anger, or fear may still be present, but I am no longer anxious, angry, or afraid.

As powerful as hagah practice is, it is limited to my own awakening. A similar practice but one that focuses on the well-being of others is found in the Buddhist practice of *metta*, a Pali word that means "gentle" and "friend" and which has come to be associated with befriending others by sending them blessings.

I understand the efficacy of metta practice in the context of the nondual nature of reality. If each life is interconnected with every life in the nondual Aliveness that is Ehyeh/YHVH/Tao/Sunyata, then it might be possible for one life "here" to influence another life "there" since both "here" and "there" are part of a greater seamless reality.

While the version of metta that I practice comes from Reb Zalman, my understanding of metta comes from Sharon Salzberg, co-founder of Insight Meditation Center:

---

[18] Easwaran, *The Mantram Handbook,* 7.

We can open to everything with the healing force of love. When we feel love, our mind is expansive and open enough to include the entirety of life in full awareness, both its pleasures and its pains. We feel neither betrayed by pain nor overcome by it, and thus we can contact that which is undamaged within us regardless of the situation. Metta sees truly that our integrity is inviolate, no matter what our life situation may be. We do not need to fear anything. We are whole: our deepest happiness is intrinsic to the nature of our minds, and it is not damaged through uncertainty and change.[19]

In the *Metta Sutta* we read that "Just as a mother would protect her only child with her own life, you should cultivate boundless thoughts of lovingkindness toward all beings."[20] One way to do this to send the following thoughts toward oneself and others:

> May all beings be peaceful.
> May all beings be happy.
> May all beings be free.

There are a variety of metta phrases; these are the three I was taught. Today I practice metta with a different set of verses I learned from Reb Zalman:

> May all beings be free from fear.
> May all beings be free from compulsion.
> May all beings be blessed with love.
> May all beings be blessed with peace.

[19] Sharon Salzberg, *Lovingkindness* (Shambhala, 2002), 21-22.
[20] *Metta Sutta*, Verse 7.

While I suggest you practice metta "on the fly," reciting the verses on behalf of people you see during the day who are in distress, I also suggest you practice metta more formally at home focusing on the well-being of self, family, friends, coworkers, neighbors, and even (perhaps especially) people with whom you struggle emotionally.[21] Close your formal metta meditation with the *Discourse on Good Will* from the *Sutta Nipata*.[22]

> May all who live be filled with lasting joy.
> May deception end, and delusion cease.
> May no one despise another, nor wish them ill.
> May love grow boundless and may hatred end with
> the release of fear.

---

[21] You can find a detailed guide to the practice of metta meditation in Sharon Salzberg's *Lovingkindness*, as well as my book, *The Sacred Art of Lovingkindness* (Skylight Paths Publishing, 2006).

[22] This is my own version. A more standard translation can be found in Eknath Easwaran's *God Makes the Rivers to Flow* (Nilgiri Press, 1991), 104.

• CHAPTER 11 •

HOW TO LOVE

I define love as *the capacity to expand one's sense of self to include another in a manner that enhances the well–being of both*. According to the humanist philosopher and psychologist Erich Fromm, "Love is the answer to the problem of human existence," in that it meets humanity's deepest need: "the need to overcome separateness, to leave the prison of aloneness."[1] Torah agrees.

In the book of Genesis, each step of the process of creation is capped with this critique: *ki tov*, "it was good." The first time *lo tov*, or "it was not good," appears is in the second chapter of Genesis, when God realizes that "it is not good for the earthling (*adam* from *adamah*/earth) to be alone."[2]

Being alone is the fundamental problem of human existence, and according to both Fromm and Torah, the solution to this problem is to find someone to love, someone who can breach our aloneness without erasing our uniqueness. Realizing that it is not good for the earthling to be alone, God forms "every beast of the earth and every fowl of the air" and presents them to the

---

[1] Erich Fromm, *The Art of Loving* (HarperCollins, 1956), 7.
[2] Genesis 2:18.

earthling, to see by what names they should be called. Naming in this context is a way of reading the nature of each creature and seeing if any of them reflects the nature of adam, who is doing the naming. None did, and so "for adam there was no *ezer k'negdo*, no help-meet."[3]

To rectify this situation, God temporarily anesthetizes adam and fashions a woman from the flesh of adam's side. Upon waking and seeing what God has made, adam says, "This shall be called woman (*ishah*), for from man (*ish*) was she taken."[4]

It is important to note that Torah does not use the words *ish* and *ishah*—man and woman—until after the split of the singular adam/earthling into two beings. *Adam* was originally both male *and* female: "In the image of God, God created adam: male and female God created adam."[5]

In the fourth-century collection of rabbinic teachings called *Midrash Rabbah*, the Great Compendium of Midrash (rabbinic interpretations of the Bible), Jeremiah ben Eleazer, says that God created adam androgynous. However, Samuel ben Nachman disagrees taking the passage to mean that God created adam as conjoined twins, and then cut adam in two along the back.[6]

Given the pedagogy inherent in Jewish Mind: *elu v'elu d'vrei Elohim chayyim*, this opinion and that opinion (no matter how incompatible) are both the words of the Living God, the rabbinic tradition makes no effort to assert or refute either position. It is important to note, however, that adam, the original earthling, was singular and whole, and that the appearance of ish/man and ishah/woman resulted from a loss of this primordial wholeness.

Adam was whole (male and female), but alone, and

[3] Genesis 2:19–20.
[4] Genesis 2:21–23.
[5] Genesis 1:27.
[6] Genesis Rabbah 8:1.

aloneness, was *lo tov*, not good. Yet adam's aloneness was a consequence of his wholeness. The question Torah raises is this: can we be whole and yet not alone? According to the eleventh-century French rabbi Rashi, when God brings the animals to adam in Genesis, they arrive in pairs, male and female. It is this fact that causes adam to lament, "All of them have mates, but I have no mate." According to Rashi, it is at that moment that God separates adam into ish and ishah.[7]

The goal of this separation is a new kind of unity: "they shall be one flesh."[8] According to Rabbi Moses ben Nahman,[9] only when the ishah and ish stand opposite one another is their desire for one another kindled, and only then can they decide to become one.[10]

What adam realized as the animals came to him, each with their mate, was that love requires the unity of opposites. There is no love without a beloved to love. In other words, the Greater Aliveness of which all life is a manifestation embraces—not erases—duality in nonduality. The key word here is *embraces*.

The love that Torah defines as *ezer k'nedgo* is not a love that erases the self in service to the other, but that stands up the self over and against the other. This understanding of love is lost in the conventional—and limited—translation of ezer k'nedgo as "help–meet,"[11] implying that the female helper is subservient to the male being helped.

The phrase *ezer k'negdo* means "one who helps (*ezer*) by (*k'*) standing against or in opposition to the other (*negdo*)." Each partner is an ezer k'negdo to the other: not a subservient helper,

---

[7] Rashi on Genesis 2:20. Rashi, *The Torah with Rashi's Commentary*. Rabbi Yisrael Isser Zvi Herczeg, trans. (Mesorah Publications, 2007), 28.

[8] Genesis 2:24.

[9] Nachmanides or Ramban, 1194–1270.

[10] Ramban, *The Torah with Ramban's Commentary*, Rabbi Yaakov Blinder, trans. (Mesorah Publications, 2009), 117.

[11] Genesis 2:18

but one who takes on the role of loyal or loving opposition. The role of the ezer k'negdo is to stand in opposition to the beloved when the beloved is about to do something contrary to the well-being of self and other.

The mission of humanity, according to Torah, is to "serve and protect"[12] nature and to "be a blessing to all the families of the earth."[13] The role of an ezer k'negdo is to stand in loving opposition to one's beloved to help the other fulfill that mission. This is what Thich Nhat Hanh calls "helping our hearts to grow."[14] One way we help a beloved's heart to grow is to show them when and where their heart is shrinking. This is what philosopher Kenneth Kramer calls "mutual stand–taking and mutual self–giving."[15] An ezer k'negdo stands against their beloved in a way that invites the beloved to transcend the limits to which they have grown comfortable.

From the perspective of Zen Mind/Jewish Mind, "true love gives us beauty, freshness, solidarity, freedom, and peace. True love includes a feeling of deep joy that we are alive. If we don't feel this way when we feel love, then it's not true love.... The other person always deserves your full respect." [16] And this respect love means standing up to the other to help them achieve their highest moral goals.

> Love integrates what is disintegrating, unites what is separated, weakens and annihilates the egoistic isolation, replaces struggle for existence by harmonious unity, co–operation, and mutual aid. In this way

[12] Genesis 2:15.
[13] Genesis 12:3.
[14] Nhat Hanh, *How to Love* (Parallax Press, 2015), 8.
[15] Kenneth Kramer, *Martin Buber's I and Thou: Practicing Living Dialogue* (Paulist Press, 2003), 23.
[16] Nhat Hanh, *How to Love*, 11-12.

it tends to make the whole universe one harmonious cosmos in which each particle is not fighting all the others but harmoniously working with the rest of the world. [17]

[17] Pitrim A. Sorokin, *Explorations in Altruistic Love and Behavior* (Beacon Press, 1950), 14.

• CHAPTER 12 •

HOW TO FIGHT

In *How to Fight*, Thich Nhat Hanh writes, "When someone says something unkind to you, you may want to retaliate right away. That is where the fight begins. This habitual way of reacting creates a well-worn pathway in your brain…. One millisecond [on this pathway] is enough for you to arrive at the same destination: anger and a desire to punish the person who has dared to make you suffer."[1]

Buddhist author Robert Thurman writes,

> Anger is a deadly sin, a destructive addiction, and a major cause of crime and death—but only when its fiery energy is misdirected by delusion, the false absolutization of self and others. This places us in a futile rage against the universe (as if the universe has nothing better to do than go after us).
>
> The egocentric, alienated person thinks this impossible situation can be solved by pumping up the self to destroy the universe. But that's like Brer

[1] Thich Nhat Hanh, *How to Fight* (Parallax Press, 2017), 10.

> Rabbit attacking the Tar-Baby, trying to break free but only getting more and more stuck. Anger's wild energy is not the problem. It is simply raw energy. When directed by wisdom instead of delusion, it can be turned against the real bars of the prison, namely, the delusions that falsely separate us from the universe.[2]

It is the isolated self, the self Jewish Mind calls *mochin d'kat-nut*, narrow mind, that suffers and seeks retribution in anger and the actions anger sanctions. We are of course talking about destructive anger, and the way to cool such anger is, according to Thich Nhat Hanh, the practice of mindfulness.

> [M]indfulness can help us pause for a moment and become aware of the anger building up in us. Stopping gives us a chance to acknowledge and to transform our anger. When we feel anger, irritation, or indignation arising in us, we pause. We stop and come back to our breathing straight away. We do not say or do anything when we are inhabited by this kind of energy, so we don't escalate the conflict. We wait until we're calm again. Being able to pause is the greatest gift.[3]

This is the way of Zen Mind. The way of Jewish Mind is articulated by the thirteenth-century Spanish mystic Rabbi Moshe ben Nachman (also called Ramban and Nachmanides, 1194-1270) in a letter he wrote to his son in 1267 at the age

---

[2] Robert Thurman cited in Rami Shapiro, *Sacred Art of Loving Kindness* (SkyLight Paths, 2006), 131-32.

[3] Nhat Hanh, *How to Fight*, 12.

of twenty, which is today called *Iggeret HaRamban*, the Letter of Ramban. Here is my interpretive rendition of *Iggeret HaRamban*:

> Listen carefully to the discipline of your father and do not abandon the guidance of your mother[4] for in this way both reason and wisdom will guide you.[5] Always speak gently to all people, and in time gentleness will become a habit and protect you from anger.
>
> Anger is dangerous and leads to grievous error, clouding your judgment, mistaking your desires for divine command, and replacing the Ehyeh/I Alone am of YHVH with "I am alone" of ego.
>
> Our rabbis taught, "Whoever flares up in anger is subject to the delusion of Hell: [6] the delusion of being "apart from" when in fact you are always "a part of" the One Who is all. Caught in this delusion, you are trapped in the hell of alienation, filling the imagined loss of God by worshipping the self. Thus, it is written, "Banish anger from your heart and remove evil from your flesh."[7] The evil of the heart is the delusion of separation, the evil of the flesh is the idolatry of worshipping oneself and one's tribe.
>
> You banish evil by cultivating humility for "on the heels of humility comes the wonder of God."[8] The wonder of God is the realization that all life is

---

[4] Proverbs 1:8.

[5] Compare this to Lao Tzu's advice: Know the masculine and keep to the feminine" in verse 28 of the *Tao te Ching*.

[6] Talmud, *Nedarim* 22a.

[7] Ecclesiastes 11:10.

[8] Proverbs 22:4.

the happening of YHVH. Knowing this you know you are a part of all life and never apart from or greater than any other life. It is this sense of humility that reminds you of the One in Whom your life and all life unfolds—the Fountain of Glory of Whom it is written, "Behold heaven and the heaven of heavens cannot contain You,[9] certainly not the hearts of humankind."[10]

This Fountain of Glory is YHVH, the infinite and formless Aliveness Who manifests the finite forms of life. This is the I AM in whom we say "I am." Everything is from YHVH and of YHVH, for there is only YHVH. Thus, it is written, "Do I [YHVH] not fill heaven and earth?"[11] *Ein od milvado*: there is nothing else.[12]

One who pretends to be superior to another, rebels against God, for there are no others, only God. If you have wealth and honor know that "wealth and honor come from God."[13] If you are wise, know that "time robs even the most eloquent sages of their wisdom."[14] You were born not for your own ends, but to serve and protect the world,[15] and to be a blessing to all the families of the earth.[16]

All people stand as equals before God. Speak gently to all beings. When you meet another, nod your head in humble recognition of the One

---

[9] 1 Kings 8:27.
[10] 2 Chronicles 6:18.
[11] Jeremiah 23:24.
[12] Deuteronomy 4:35.
[13] 1 Chronicles 29:12.
[14] Job 12:20.
[15] Genesis 2:15.
[16] Genesis 12:3.

manifest in all. Cast your heart heavenward, opening to the wonder of God who is the Source and Substance of all. When speaking, do not stare at your listener to intimidate, but rather look at them with compassion to invite conversation.

In thought, word, and deed know you are standing in the presence of the Holy One, and that the Shekhinah, the Feminine Divine rests upon you always. Indeed, the glory of God fills the cosmos.[17]

Speak reverently and with awe, ready to serve the way of righteousness. Act with restraint in the company of others. If one should taunt you, do not answer defensively, but respond gently in tones that invite dialogue and connection. Take care to turn Torah diligently so that you will discover Her wisdom for perfecting the world with justice, kindness, and humility. When you arise from your turning, ponder carefully what you have learned; see what there is in it that you can put into practice. For there is little point in learning without living. Learn in order to transform the world and yourself with justice and compassion.

Read this letter weekly and walk forever in the ways of God. In this way, you will succeed in your endeavors, for all you desire will be for the good of all. *Amen, Selah!*

---

[17] Isaiah 6:3; Psalms 19:1.

• CHAPTER 13 •

HOW TO FORGIVE

While I mentioned forgiveness briefly in chapter 4, it is worth revisiting. Forgiveness isn't something you bestow or receive; forgiveness is something that simply arises when you understand the nature of reality as *tohu va-vohu*: wild, chaotic, and fundamentally beyond your control.[1]

Because life is tohu va-vohu, suffering happens. Because life is tohu va-vohu, joy happens. Because life is tohu va-vohu, suffering and joy often happen together. And none of this happens *to* you—or to anyone else. Rather, all of this happens *with* you and everyone else. To imagine that life happens to you is to imagine that life is other than you, but there is nothing other, there is only Ehyeh/YHVH/Tao/Sunyata. This is the meaning of interbeing, nonduality: every happening happens with every other happening as a manifesting of the only happening there is: Ehyeh/YHVH/Tao/Sunyata.

Amid the uncontrollable chaos of tohu va-vohu, things are said and done that cannot be avoided. This is expressed beautifully in the great sixth-century Buddhist teacher Sen Ts'an's *Hsin*

[1] Genesis 1:2.

Hsin Ming/ Trust in Mind: "The Great Way is easy for those who have no preferences. When love and hate are both irrelevant to you, everything becomes clear and obvious."

It isn't that Zen Mind/Jewish Mind never experiences preferences, but that it doesn't cling to those preferences. I value love over hate, but in the uncontrollable wildness of any given moment, love and hate happen of their own accord: they happen *with* me rather than *to* me or *by* me. This is so because there is no "me" separate from tohu va-vohu.

Zen Mind/Jewish Mind isn't about erasing the difference between love and hate, good and evil, justice and injustice. Rather, Zen Mind/Jewish Mind is about realizing that all such opposites are irreducible expressions of the greater nondual reality, the generative tissue that is Ehyeh/YHVH/Tao/Sunyata. This is what the author of the parable of the Tree of Knowledge tries to tell us when she[2] has good and evil arise from the same tree.

People want to be happy and will do lots of stupid things to make themselves happy. Sometimes our quest to be happy makes other people sad, but most people don't set out to deliberately hurt you. Most people get caught up in the pursuit of their own happiness, and then are as surprised as you are when their pursuit causes you pain.

Often, when we set out to make ourselves happy, we mentally script a play, and then try to encourage, convince, manipulate, or force others to act out the parts we have written for them. This rarely works. People refuse to read their lines, or take their places, or let you have your way. They have their own scripts from which they want *you* to read, and they have committed themselves to their own preferred outcomes. It's a mess.

---

[2] I am persuaded by Harold Bloom's argument that the author of the early stories about YHVH in Genesis were written by women. See Harold Bloom, *The Book of J* (Grove Press, 2004).

But there is an alternative: stop trying to script your life and just go about living it.

Zen Mind/Jewish Mind lives with not-knowing. Zen Mind/Jewish Mind understands that life is wild and chaotic and outside our—or anyone's—control. And Zen Mind/Jewish Mind knows that forgiveness happens when we realize that, most of the time, people are not out to get us, but are out to take care of themselves. True, sometimes their caretaking causes us pain and suffering, but with the exceptions of sociopaths and other people with personality disorders, our pain and suffering are collateral damage, not the point of their actions. The point is happiness, even though the results are often suffering.

Zen Mind/Jewish Mind lives life as tohu va-vohu. When life is painful, feel the pain. When it is joyous, feel the joy. As King Solomon reminds us in the Book of Ecclesiastes:

> Everything in this world has its moment,
> a time of ripening and falling away:
> Moments of birthing and moments of dying.
> Moments of planting and moments of reaping.
> Moments of killing and moments of healing.
> Moments of demolishing and moments of building.
> Moments of weeping and moments of laughing.
> Moments of mourning and moments of dancing.
> Moments of scattering stones and moments of gathering stones.
> Moments of embracing and moments of distancing.
> Moments of seeking and moments of losing.
> Moments of clinging and moments of releasing.
> Moments of tearing and moments of mending.
> Moments of silence and moments of talking.
> Moments of loving and moments of hating.

Moments of warring and moments of peacemaking.[3]

The key is *not* to avoid or minimize the negative moments and embrace and maximize the positive moments. The key is to recognize what moment you are in and to live accordingly. But you can't do that if you're tied to a script about what life should be and weighed down with past hurts and ever-present grudges. This is why forgiveness is crucial to right living: it frees you from the past so that you can fully engage the present, both good and bad.

To explore living from tohu va-vohu, experiment with my version of Reb Nachman of Breslov's nightly forgiveness prayer:

> Knowing the wildness and uncontrollability of both moment and mind; knowing how easily the self becomes entrapped in suffering, and how its desperate attempt to alleviate that suffering often results in causing suffering to others, I forgive anyone who brought me suffering today. I forgive them whether this was done freely or under duress, consciously or unconsciously, accidentally or on purpose. May my gift of forgiveness alleviate the other's suffering and may no one be hurt because of me. May I be a blessing to all the families of the earth, that the world might be a better place for my being born into her. May the words of my mouth and the meditations of my heart be translated into the actions of my hands. Amen.

Again: life is wild and chaotic and out of your control: a constant flow of temporary moments, some wondrous and

---

[3] Ecclesiastes 3:1-8.

some horrible. And you and everyone else are included in that happening. Nothing happens *to* you; everything happens *with* you. And because there is no point to any of this, other than to be precisely what it is, there is no thought of reward or punishment. There is just what to do in and with this moment, and the next one.

When you know this, forgiveness just happens, because forgiveness isn't about making peace with the last moment, but about making room for the next moment.

• CHAPTER 14 •

HOW TO THANK

For me, the most powerful way to cultivate gratitude is through the practice of *Naikan* (Japanese for "inner seeing"). Naikan was developed by Yoshimoto Ishin (1916–88), a follower of Jodo Shinshu, or Pure Land Buddhism.

A central practice of Pure Land is *mishirabe*, Critical Review (*Shirabe*) of Self (*Mi*). This is a practice of self-reflection in which you recall how specific people, beginning with your mother, have helped you throughout your life, and the debt you owe them for doing so. In time, you realize the enormity of your debt, and the desire to repay it by giving to others.

Naikan secularizes the practice of mishirabe, and today it is accepted as a legitimate form of psychotherapy in Japan. It was introduced to the United States by my teacher, Dr. David Reynolds.

My Naikan training occurred throughout a ten-day retreat. I spent a major part of each day alone, asking myself three questions regarding the people in my life, beginning with my mother:

1) What has my mother done for me?

2) What have I done for my mother?

3) What trouble have I caused my mother?

Mishirabe is practiced in reverse chronological order. In other words, you first ask yourself these questions about the past year, and then ask them of each prior year, as far back as your memory allows. When you have completed your review of your life with your mother, you move on to other key people: your father, siblings, friends, teachers, partner, etc. By the end of the retreat, if the practice is going well, you are overwhelmed by the giftedness of your life. Your sense of being loved and cared for is so strong that you can only respond by loving and caring for others.

While I place a great deal of value in this way of practicing mishirabe, my daily Naikan practice follows a broader formula taught by my friends Linda Anderson Krech and her husband Greg. Each night as I lie in bed, I ask myself the following three questions:

What did I receive from the world today? This includes any benefits that I received from other people, animals, nature, inanimate objects, technology, organizations, etc.

What did I give to the world today? This includes any way that the world benefited from my presence on Earth during the past twenty-four hours.

What troubles did I cause the world today? This includes both troubles that were deliberate and controllable and troubles that were accidental and uncontrollable.

When I find myself answering the question, *What troubles did the world cause me today?*—then, as I was taught, I just let those answers drift away and return to the three questions.[1]

Each night, I discover that I was gifted by others far more than I gifted others, and the troubles I caused usually outweighed them both. With daily Naikan comes a desire to repay my debt by gifting others tomorrow. Oddly enough, the more I seek to repay my debt, the deeper my indebtedness becomes. This is not unique, as this anecdote told by David Reynolds makes clear.

As a psychotherapist David used to split his therapy practice between the United States and Japan, spending six months per year in each country. When in the U.S. he lived in a run-down neighborhood in Los Angeles, providing therapy to those who could not otherwise afford it. On one corner of his block was a gas station, and next to the gas station was a lot strewn with trash. As a way of showing gratitude to his neighbors, David decided to spend a Saturday cleaning up the lot.

The lot was owned by the proprietor of the gas station. David spoke to the man earlier in the week and explained that he would like to clean up the lot on Saturday. At first, the man was suspicious, but David convinced him that he had no intent of doing harm, and the gas station owner agreed.

That Saturday David walked over to the lot wearing a pair of gardening gloves and carrying a pile of trash bags, and set about picking up the trash. About thirty minutes into this venture, the owner of the station showed up with a broom handle he had fitted with a nail on one end. "Use this to pick up the papers," the man said, "It'll be easier on your back." David

---

[1] Linda Anderson Krech, "You Can't Control Depression, But What Can You Do? *Thirty Thousand Days: A Journal for Purposeful Living*, Vol. 23, no. 3, 11.

smiled appreciatively and took the broom handle. But inwardly he was disappointed. The whole idea of cleaning the lot was to pay his neighbors back for being kind to him. Now he was incurring a new debt to the gas station owner. Things went downhill from there.

About an hour later, the gas station owner appeared again. This time he had his own broom handle with a nail on the end, and he set about helping David clean the lot. Of course, this made the job easier, but it made the debt greater. Worse still, other neighbors noticed what the two men were doing and came out to join them. People came out to help clean the lot, provide water and food for the workers, and haul the trash away to a dumpster. The harder he worked to pay off his debt to his neighbors, the harder his neighbors worked to help him deepen it.

Of course, they had no idea they were interfering with David's plan. They only noticed a person helping to make their neighborhood better, and spontaneously came out to help. This is how the world works when you practice Naikan. The more aware you are of the help you receive the more you try to give back, and the more you give back the more help you invite.

Often when I share this story, someone says to me, "OK, I get it. You're trying to make me feel guilty. Well, guilt isn't exactly a motivator for me." But Naikan isn't about guilt at all. It's about gratitude.

One afternoon toward the end of my Naikan training, David and I were talking in the kitchen. Noticing the faucet of the kitchen sink was dripping, he walked over to the sink, tightened the faucet, and stopped the dripping. There was nothing special in his action, yet I felt compelled to ask, "Why did you do that?"

"I owed it to the faucet," he said. "The faucet is designed to carry water into the kitchen sink for our benefit. In a sense, it wants to do its job to the best of its ability. Not tightening the faucet and allowing it to drip is an act of disrespect. So, out of respect, I shut it off properly."

"There are lots of good reasons to shut off a dripping faucet," I said. "It saves water; the dripping sound grates on the nerves; but you went with respect."

"Saving water and soothing nerves isn't Naikan," he said. "Respect is Naikan. Saving water serves me. Respecting the faucet serves the faucet. It's a way to say, 'Thank you for bringing me water when I want and need it.'"

"That's Naikan?" I asked.

"That's Naikan," David said.

You don't have to feel gratitude for everything. You don't have to be grateful for having terminal cancer. You don't have to be grateful to the drunk driver who slammed into your car and left you unable to walk. You don't have to be grateful for the shit you step in, or the cancer that is stealing the life of someone you love—or your own.

Still, I have seen people at death's door take a moment and thank those who have loved them and cared for them. I have seen people who, at the moment of their death, give thanks for having lived. I have seen people suffering from incurable and terminal illnesses reach out to others in the same situation and offer a helping hand and a listening ear.

We are gifted right up to the moment of our death. And the responsibility of giving thanks for those gifts ends only when the last breath leaves our body.

Like every other aspect of Zen Mind/Jewish Mind, gratitude is natural when you see the world as it truly is. It comes naturally when you treat another human being—or any other being or object—as a manifesting of Ehyeh/YHVH/Tao/Sunyata. Like forgiveness, gratitude comes naturally when you realize the true nature of this and every moment as a happening of the One who is happening as all.

• CHAPTER 15 •

HOW TO REST

"People are waking up to the truth of their manipulation under toxic systems. People are waking up to heal. People are waking up to rest. We will no longer be a martyr for grind culture. Grind culture is a collaboration between white supremacy and capitalism. It views our divine bodies as machines. Our worth is not connected to how much we produce. Another way is possible."[1]

Another way was invented by pre-capitalist brown people in the wilderness of Sinai some 3,000 years ago. They were called Israelites then, Jews today, and their other way was and is *Shabbat*. The Jewish Sabbath was infuriating to many, seeing rightly that Shabbat is an act of resistance to the culture built on exploitation of labor. As Tricia Hersey, the author of the previous paragraph so accurately points out: rest is resistance and "our collective rest will change the world because our rest resides in a Spirit of refusal and disruption. Rest is our protest. Rest is resistance. Rest is reparations."[2]

---

[1] Tricia Hersey, *Rest is Resistance: A Manifesto* (Little, Brown Spark, 2022), 12.
[2] Hersey, *Rest is Resistance*, 12.

Rest as resistance, disruption, and protest is Shabbat, and it is made all the more powerful because it is done in a state of joy and play rather than anger and outcry.

Shabbat was so troubling to the powers that be that they invented outrageous origins for the practice in hopes of defeating it. My favorite is recorded by the Jewish historian Josephus who records the theory of Apion, a Greco-Egyptian grammarian, who insisted that the Sabbath was the result of jock itch. After six days of wandering in the Sinai, Apion imagined, the Israelites developed an inflammation of the groin the Egyptians called *Sabbatosia* from which the Israelites derived the word Shabbat.[3] Sadly for Apion, the idea of Shabbat predates the exodus from Egypt and is linked to the seventh day of creation: "God rested on the seventh day from all the work that God had done. So God blessed the seventh day and set it apart [from the six days of labor], because on that day god rested from all the work of creating."[4]

The Hebrew Bible makes it clear that the Jews too found it difficult to break their addiction to work. The Prophet Amos chides the people's yearning for the end of the Sabbath Day so they could get back to selling wheat,[5] and when the Jews return to Judah from exile in Babylonia (fifth century BCE) their governor Nehemiah scolds the leadership for profaning the Sabbath by not protecting the idea of rest.[6]

Rest as resistance, however, is not unique to the Jews. In a parable attributed to the Taoist sage Chuang Tzu, a wealthy passerby accosts a fisherman resting in his boat in the early afternoon.

---

[3] Josephus, *Against Apion*, II, 3.
[4] Genesis 2:2-3.
[5] Amos 8:5.
[6] Nehemiah 13:17.

"Why aren't you out fishing?" the passerby asks.

"I've caught enough for the day," the fisherman replies.

"But why not catch more than enough? Certainly, the fish haven't retired for the day!"

"What would I do with the extra fish?" the fisherman asks.

"That's obvious! You could sell them, buy a better boat, improve your nets, maybe hire more help and purchase more boats. In time you could be as rich as me!"

"What would I do then?" the fisherman asks.

"Why then you could relax and enjoy life!"

"Which is what I am doing right now," said the fisherman.

In the world of Chuang Tzu, "fish symbolize fertility, strength, prosperity, freedom, and joy,"[7] and the parable is a critique of the ceaseless pursuit of such things. In our world, it is a critique of the ceaseless pursuit of ceaseless pursuing. This is what capitalism is: the ceaseless pursuit of capital for its own sake. What upsets the wealthy passerby is the fisherman's refusal to play along.

I imagine his upset is made all the more acute by the fact that the fisherman isn't actively fighting the economic system of the passerby and seeking to overthrow it with an alternative system but is rather taking refuge in the Tao. Water represents Tao and the attributes of "purity, transparency, reflectivity, passivity, formlessness, humility, fluidity, receptivity, and fertility. Thus,

---

[7] Krill Ole Thompson, "What Is the Reason of Failure or Success?" in Roger T. Ames, *Wandering at Ease in the Zhuangzi* (SUNY Press, 1998), 17.

contemplative fishermen in long contact with such waters will spontaneously awaken to *dao* [Tao]." [8]

In the context of Zen Mind/Jewish Mind Tao is the infinite and infinitely creative and fecund field of Ehyeh/YHVH/Tao/Sunyata from which and in which all life arises and returns. The fisherman in this parable is one who takes refuge in What Is (*koach mah* a pun on the word *chochma*/wisdom in Hebrew, *tathata*/suchness in Sanskrit) rather than straining to make it over into what it should be.

Decades ago, while on retreat at the original Elat Chayyim Jewish retreat center in upstate New York, I stood on a wooden bridge contemplating a stream flowing beneath me. Something was amiss. The rocks and logs that shaped the water's flow were off somehow. I climbed down into the stream and adjusted them. Returning to my perch on the bridge I assessed my renovations. Still not right, I returned to the stream and adjusted some more. I did this over and again until it dawned on me that I was playing God. On Shabbat. I bowed low to the stream, apologized to the rocks and logs, and walked on laughing at my foolishness.

Six days a week you shall play God, but on the seventh day you shall remember that God is playing you.

Of course, as Thich Nhat Hanh teaches, "You don't need to set aside special time for resting and relaxing. You don't need a special pillow or any fancy equipment. You don't need a whole hour. In fact, now is a very good time to relax,"[9] but I'm the kind of person who benefits from special times for resting. Shabbat is that time.

> If you want to enter the holiness of the day you must
> first lay down the profanity of clattering commerce,

[8] Krill Ole Thompson, "What Is the Reason of Failure or Success?" in Roger T. Ames, *Wandering at Ease in the Zhuangzi*, Albany: SUNY Press, 1998, p. 18.
[9] Thich Nhat Hanh, *How to Relax* (Parallax Press, 2015), 6.

of being yoked to toil. You must go away from the screech of dissonant days, from the nervousness and fury of acquisitiveness and the betrayal in embezzling your own life. You must say farewell to manual work and learn to understand that the world has already been created and will survive without the help of humankind.[10]

Rabbi Heschel's phrase "the yoke of toil" is central to understanding the revolutionary nature of Shabbat. The English word "yoke" is connected to the Sanskrit word *yuj* from which comes the word yoga. What I hear Rabbi Heschel saying is that on the seventh day we should set aside the yoga of work and take up the yoga of Shabbat, the yoga of rest. For me, the yoga of Shabbat is the yoga of the resting fisherman. Just as the fisherman took refuge by the waters of Tao, so the Shabbat yogi takes refuge in YHVH and the qualities of Shabbat: "tranquility, serenity, peace, and repose."[11]

While Judaism has many rules regarding Shabbat, I suggest you play with them as you choose. I prefer principles to rules when it comes to Shabbat, and my guiding principle for Shabbat is the Chinese ideal of *wu wei*, non-coercive action.

> *Wu wei* is often translated as "not doing," "not acting," or "not interfering," but "not forcing" seems to me to hit the nail on the head. We never force a lock because we will bend the key or break the lock. Instead, we jiggle it until it turns. *Wu wei* means always acting in accord with the pattern of things as they exist. When we follow the principles of *wu wei* we do not impose any kind of extraneous force on

[10] Abraham Joshua Heschel, *The Sabbath* (Farrar, Straus and Giroux, 1951), 13.
[11] *Genesis Rabbah* 10:9, cited in Heschel, *The Sabbath*, 13.

a situation, because such force, by its very nature, is not in accord with the situation.[12]

I begin Shabbat on Friday evening with the lighting of two Shabbat candles. Before the lighting I read the following:

> I take the time to make this day a sabbath. I set aside the labors that define me and uncover the Aliveness that cannot be defined.
>
> May these hours of rest and renewal open my heart to joy and my mind to truth. May all who struggle find rest on this day. May all who suffer find solace on this day. May all who hurt find healing on this day. May all who despair find purpose on this day. May all who hunger find fulfillment on this day. And may I live my life in such a way that this day may fulfill its promise.
>
> Where the world is dark with illness, let me kindle the light of healing. Where the world is bleak with suffering, let me kindle the light of caring. Where the world is dimmed by lies, let me kindle the light of truth.
>
> Wondrous is the awakening kindled by these Shabbat lights, revealing the unity of each life in the greater Aliveness that is all life.

I then do my best to spend Shabbat as Torah instructs us:

> Remember the sabbath day and protect its holiness. Six days you may labor and accomplish all your tasks, but the seventh day is a sabbath devoted to

[12] Alan Watts, *Talking Zen* (Shambhala Publications, 2022), 134-35.

YHVH. On it you shall abstain from all manner of work: you, your children, your employees, your livestock, and even foreigners who sojourn among you; for in six days YHVH created sky, earth, and sea and all that is in them, and on the seventh day YHVH rested; YHVH blessed the seventh day and hallowed it.[13]

Remember that you were enslaved in Egypt, and YHVH brought you out of your enslavement with a mighty hand and an outstretched arm; and for this reason, YHVH commands you to keep the Sabbath.[14]

Neither rationale—rest or liberation— takes precedence over the other. You honor rest when you allow yourself, your families, your employees, foreigners, and your animals to abstain from the obligatory labors of the work week, and you honor liberation when you use your rest to engage in activities that facilitate your exodus from Egypt, *Mitzrayim* in Hebrew: the narrow places of enslavement.

Mitzrayim is comprised of two Hebrew words: *mi*/from and *tzarim*/narrowness: Mitzrayim refers not only to the land of Egypt, but to the narrow places of your own life: the places of constriction and enslavement. When you free yourself from narrowness, you free yourself for true rest and liberation. This happens both physically and psychologically.

Physically you free yourself from narrowness by spending Shabbat "as if all your work were done."[15] Psychologically you free yourself from narrowness by shifting from *mochin d'katnut*, narrow mind, to *mochin d'gadlut*, spacious mind. Mochin d'gadlut

---

[13] Exodus 20:7-10.
[14] Deuteronomy 5:14.
[15] *Mekhilta, Masekhta Ba-Hodesh.*

is the Self freed from the need to have and free for the grace of sheer being.

There is much more to Shabbat rest, however, than abstaining from work.

> [Shabbat rest is] the re-establishment of complete harmony between human beings and between them and nature. Nothing must be destroyed and nothing built: the Shabbat is a day of truce in the human battle with the world.... On the Shabbat one lives as if one has nothing, pursuing no aim except being, that is, expressing one's essential powers: praying, studying, eating, drinking, singing, making love. The Shabbat is a day of joy because on that day one is fully oneself.[16]

My work is never done. Whether it is my work as a writer, podcast host, retreat leader, teacher, spouse, father, or grandfather, there is always something that needs doing. But on Shabbat I pretend otherwise: I live *as if* my work were done. This means living without deadlines, without goals, without concern for outcomes. In other words: play.

Shabbat is a day of joy for me because Shabbat is a day of play. This play is not limited by the rabbinic rules pertaining to Shabbat, but to those actions that bring me joy without precluding the joy of others. When you play simply to play rather than to win, you are engaged in Shabbat. When you converse simply to share ideas, rather than to convince someone else of the rightness of those ideas, you are engaged in Shabbat. When you act without coercion, you are engaged in Shabbat. Shabbat has no point—which, paradoxically, is the point.

[16] Erich Fromm, *To Have or to Be* (Harper & Row, 1976), 50-51.

One of my favorite Shabbat practices is walking. As the sages put it, "You should walk on Shabbat with an unhurried gait."[17] I walk miles every day, often with my dog. On most days I walk wearing a pedometer, and my goal is to walk five to seven miles each day. But on Shabbat I walk simply to walk. I put aside my concern with heart rate and step count. I walk because walking for me is a joyous activity that needs no goal outside itself.[18] I am not seeking to gain anything from my walking other than the joy of putting one foot in front of the other. And when I walk this way, I find I am walking on holy ground, ground that is the happening of YHVH. In this way my walking embodies the principal idea of Shabbat: "a state of union between human and nature and between human and human."[19]

My Shabbat is a time free from competition, even friendly competition. It is a day for living fearlessly and taking care not to frighten others.

What you do on Shabbat is up to you. You may engage in a more traditional form of Shabbat observance or a more innovative form. The key is to make your Shabbat a day of joyous play, deep rest, and revolutionary resistance to all that enslaves you and all the families of the earth.

---

[17] Talmud, Shabbat 113a.

[18] I find it intriguing and instructive that the Hebrew word for Jewish law is *halacha* from the word *halach*, to walk. Halacha is the way a Jew walks in the world.

[19] Erich Fromm, *To Have Or To Be*. NY: Harper & Row, 1976, p. 197, adapted.

• CHAPTER 16 •

HOW TO WALK

I mentioned walking for walking's sake in the previous chapter. Here I want to share walking as a formal meditative practice: a means of shedding the delusion of separateness from Ehyeh/YHVH/Tao/Sunyata and realizing that all life is a manifesting of the aliveness that is Ehyeh/YHVH/Tao/Sunyata. The practice is called *lech lecha*, walking toward your Self.

In his book, *How to Walk*, Thich Nhat Hanh writes:

> The first thing to do is to lift your foot. Breathe in.
> Put your foot down in front of you, first your heel
> and then your toes. Breathe out. Feel your feet solid
> on the Earth. You have already arrived.[1]

Decades ago, when I was a congregational rabbi, I introduced *kinhin*, Zen walking meditation, to my community and we eventually planted a large flower garden designed for walking practice. The garden was accessible at all hours, but we

---

[1] Thich Nhat Hanh, *How to Walk* (Parallax Press, 2015), 7.

specifically encouraged people to walk the garden before entering the synagogue to pray as a way of emptying themselves of themselves in preparation for prayer.

I reached out to Thich Nhat Hanh and requested a blessing we could use to dedicate the garden he had inspired. He did far more than that and sent a Vietnamese nun of his Order of Interbeing to teach us kinhin in our walking meditation garden. Regretfully I no longer remember the sister's name, but I do remember how delightful she was, and how authentic was her walking practice. Maybe too authentic.

The congregation had prepared a kosher-vegetarian Shabbat dinner at the synagogue to welcome her. We sent several congregants to meet her at Miami International Airport and bring her to our shul in plenty of time to eat before Shabbat.

Our members were at the airport on time. Her plane landed on time. And she joined them on time. But her Buddhist time was not our Jewish time. With her roller bag and my congregants in tow, Sister walked mindfully through the airport to the car: breathing in; putting one foot down in front of the other, heel to toe; breathing out; feeling their feet solid on the floor; they had already arrived. Arrived, yes. Just not at the synagogue. Sister's karma was good, however, and she did arrive in time to eat something, introduce us to kinhin, and deepen our walking practice as she shared Shabbat and the rest of the weekend with us.

The Jewish version of kinhin is called *Lech Lecha* and comes from Genesis 12:1:

> YHVH said to Avram and Sarai, "*lech lecha* from your country, your kin, and your parents' home to a land a will show you."

Conventionally, the Hebrew *lech lecha* is translated as "go forth," and the passage is read as a command to leave home and journey to a distant land. As with most conventional readings of Torah, this one too misses the deeper spiritual teaching of the text. The literal reading of the Hebrew is *lech*/walk *le*/toward *cha*/yourself. What is usually read as a call to make an outer journey, is in fact a call to make an inner one, supported by the direction God sets for Avram and Sarai: "*lech lecha* from your country, your kin, and your parents' home."

If Avram and Sarai (soon to be renamed Avraham and Sarah) were called to an outer journey, logic dictates that they would first take leave of their parents' home, then the land occupied by their kinfolk, and lastly the larger geographical area of the country in which their kinfolk live. Yet YHVH commands the exact opposite. Why? Because this is not an outer physical journey but an inner psychological one, and the order of departure points represents the difficulty of liberation. It is easier to leave your attachment to nationality than your attachment to ethnicity, culture, and religion, and it is easier to leave your attachment to ethnicity, culture, and religion than it is to leave your attachment to family, race, sex, and gender. Yet the call to arrive at your true Self requires you free yourself from all of this.

Without all such narratives only Ehyeh, the nondual I Am remains. This is the I Am of Buddha when he responds to the Brahmin Dona's query "What sort of being are you?" saying "I am awake."[2] This is the I am of the Jew Jesus when he says, "I am the way, the truth, and the life."[3] And this is the I am of you when you speak free from the narratives that blind you to your true Self.

You don't become this I Am. You are this I Am. As Thich Nhat Hanh says, you have already arrived. It isn't a matter of

[2] Dona Sutta, 4:36.
[3] John 14:6.

getting someplace, but of realizing every place as *HaMakom*, The Place, an ancient rabbinic name for YHVH derived from the Hebrew root *mem-kuf-mem* meaning "existence." YHVH is the infinite place in which all existence happens. As the twelfth-century Jewish philosopher Maimonides wrote, "YHVH doesn't have a place inside or outside the universe, rather YHVH is The Place/*HaMakom* of the universe."[4]

My Lech Lecha practice builds on the teaching of Thich Nhat Hanh: as you breathe and place each foot on the ground, ask yourself: "Who is aware of this body walking?" As feelings arise in your awareness, ask yourself: "Who is aware of these feelings?" As thoughts arise in your awareness, ask yourself: "Who is aware of these thoughts?" As awareness of being aware arises in your mind, ask yourself: "Who is aware of being aware?" Over time you will realize that just outside the field of awareness and the act of asking is a greater consciousness that disappears every time you look for it. To borrow from the Brihadaranyaka Upanishad, the Seer sees but cannot be seen. This unseen and unseeable Seer is the I Am manifesting all reality.

> Walking brings the mind and body together. Only when mind and body are united are we truly in the here and now. When we walk, we come home to ourselves. If you're busy talking while you walk, or planning ahead, you won't enjoy your in-breath and out-breath. You won't enjoy being fully in the present moment.[5]

Coming home to ourselves is a perfect translation of lech lecha. Home is "the land I will show you", the land revealed by

---

[4] Moses Maimonides, *Commentary on Mishnah, Sanhedrin* 10:3.
[5] Nhat Hanh, *How to Walk*, 57.

Ehyeh/YHVH/Tao/Sunyata to be the very Place/HaMakom you happen to be at this and every moment. God doesn't provide a map for this journey because the journey isn't geographical but psychological. Lech Lecha is not about finding the right map, but about setting aside all maps—all isms and ideologies—and being present to HaMakom.

But don't imagine that being present is the point. The point as Genesis 12:3 tells us, is to "be a blessing to all the families of the earth;" all of them—human, animal, vegetable, and mineral.

Knowing your true Self is never the point; freeing yourself is never the point. Realizing Ehyeh/YHVH/Tao/Sunyata in service to helping others do the same is the point.

• CHAPTER 17 •

HOW TO WAKE UP
(IN THE MORNING)

I once overheard Alan Lew, the ur Zen rabbi, say to some-one, "I can't teach you how to be awake, but I can share a Jewish practice for waking up." He was referring to the recitation of *Elohai nishamah* an affirmation observant Jews recite upon waking in the morning: *Elohai nishamah, sheh natata be t'horah he* which I render as "I am the pure breathing of God."[1] Let me unpack this for you.

Nishamah is one of the words for "soul" in Hebrew. It comes from the word *nishemah*/breath. Nishamah is the Hebrew equiv-alent of the Chinese *ch'i*. I take my understanding of *ch'i* from the poet and translator of Chinese texts David Hinton:

> *Ch'i* is often described as the universal life-force breathing through things. But this presumes a dual-ism that separates reality into matter and breath-force (spirit) that infuses it with life…. [C]*h'i* is both

[1] Talmud, *Berachot* 60b. The literal translation is "My God, the breath you breathe into me is pure."

ZEN MIND JEWISH MIND • 140

> life-force and matter simultaneously. It is a single
> tissue generative through and through, the matter
> and energy of the Cosmos seen together as a single
> breath-force surging through its perpetual transfor-
> mations. And so, *ch'i* is nearly synonymous with Way
> [Tao]…emphasizing [its] generative dynamism.[2]

What David Hinton says about chi is true of nishamah as well. With this understanding in mind, let's turn our attention to the notion of *t'horah*, which means "pure."

The first thing to note is that the adjective t'horah is feminine, making it clear that nishamah, the breathing of YHVH is *feminine*. The generative dynamism of YHVH is experienced as feminine in Judaism and often referred to as *Shekhinah*, a feminine noun meaning the Presence of God. Something similar can be said of Tao:

> [T]he Tao te Ching repeatedly refers to the Tao as
> mother, virgin, and womb…[speaking] directly to
> the deeply feminine nature of the Tao in Her role
> as Creator since the beginning of time…likening
> the Tao to the immortal void, a dark abyss called a
> "dark womb." She is the creator and birth-giver of
> the world, bringing forth life without effort.[3]

YHVH breathing is Tao birthing, and the nature of this breath/birth is t'horah, purity. T'horah is the absence of isms and ideologies, everything that mars our seeing of self and other as the manifesting of Ehyeh/YHVH/Tao/Sunyata.

---

[2] David Hinton, *The Way of Ch'an: Essential Texts of the Original Tradition* (Shambhala, 2023), 325.

[3] Rosemarie Anderson, *The Divine Feminine Tao te Ching: A New Translation & Commentary* (Inner Traditions, 2021), 10-11.

141 • HOW TO WAKE UP (IN THE MORNING)

When you awake in the morning, there is a moment of purity before you put on the distortions of "Jew or Gentile, slave or free, male or female."[4] You give voice to this moment when you recite *Elohai nishamah, sheh natata be t'horah he/* "I am the pure breathing of God" and realize your true nature as the pure happening of Ehyeh/YHVH/Tao/Sunyata.

> [T]he essence of Mind, the essential consciousness, is ever formless, free, and pure. "The perfect man," said Chuang-tzu, "employs his mind as a mirror; it grasps nothing, it refuses nothing, it receives, but does not keep." At the same time, this must not lead us to form the *concept* of a pure and unchanging consciousness separate and apart from the changing forms of thoughts and things. The point is not at all to reject phenomena and cling to the Absolute, because the very nature of the Absolute, of the essential Mind, is non-clinging. As soon as we conceive a formless Self or mind-essence underlying and distinct from the changing contents of experience we are denying this very nature of that Self.[5]

At the moment of waking, there is no such conceiving. Of course, this moment of waking, like all moments, is fleeting. It cannot be grasped; it can only be voiced. At the moment of wakening, before any other thought captures your imagination and triggers the inclinations, self and self-transcendence, recite *Elohai nishamah, sheh natata be t'horah he/* "I am the pure breathing of God." That is how to wake up with Zen Mind/Jewish Mind.

---

[4] Galatians 3:28.
[5] Alan Watts, *Zen: A Short Introduction* (New World Library, 2019), 48.

• CHAPTER 18 •

HOW TO SHIT

Everything is precisely as it is because Ehyeh/YHVH/ Tao/Sunyata, the happening of all happening, is as it is. Because this is so, the only intelligent way to engage with the moment is to work with the moment rather than against it. For example, when caught in a rip current your instinct is to fight your way back to shore. This will, however, exhaust you and can lead to drowning. It is wiser to swim parallel to the shore until you escape the current's pull. Working with the current rather than against it reminds you that you are part of the Happening. Nothing is happening *to* you; everything is happening *with* you. And because this is so, you can engage with what is happening in the same way a surfer engages with a wave.

While surfing involves a lot of physics, the surfer who tries to mathematically calculate how to ride any oncoming wave will fail miserably. One learns over time to ride the wave, to move intuitively on the board, and to shift one's weight unconsciously. The wave isn't happening to the surfer; the wave, wind, board, and surfer are happening together. This is yet another example of what the Chinese call *wu wei*, noncoercive action:

When your body is not aligned,
The inner power will not come.
When you are not tranquil within,
Your mind will not be well ordered.
Align your body, assist the inner power,
Then it will gradually come on its own.[1]

Aligning your body is a noncoercive act. As is aligning your mind. There is no forcing, no conflict, no violence. There is simply allowing what is to be as it is, and then to work with it as it is. This is what Alan Watts calls "getting out of your own way."

One does not stand in one's own light while working, and so the way of *wu wei* (this sounds like a pun but it isn't) is the way of non-obstruction or non-interference…

[S]uppose you are cutting wood. If you go against the way the tree grew, that is to say against the grain of the wood, the wood is very difficult to cut. If you go with the grain, however, it splits easily…. Some people are in a great hurry to get on with sawing and they try and power right through the piece. But what happens? When you turn the board over you see the back edge of the wood is full of splinters, and you find that you are rather tired as well. Any skilled carpenter will tell you, "Let the saw do the work, let the teeth do the cutting." And you find that by going at it quite easily, and just allowing the blade to glide back and forth, the wood is easily cut.[2]

[1] Harold D. Roth, *Original Tao: Inward Training* (Columbia University Press, 1999), 66.
[2] Alan Watts, *What is Tao?* (New World Library, 2000), 45-46.

What is true about surfing and sawing is true about shitting as well. Align your body with nature, get out of your own way, and let your body do what it does best when it is free to be its best.

I'm not a doctor or a homeopath and I'm not going to share tips on how to keep your body functioning optimally. But I will share with you a simple prayer for celebrating when optimal functioning occurs. It is called *Asher Yatzar*/Who has formed. As with all things Jewish, the rabbis argued over just how the prayer should be worded, but there was no doubt that some prayer of thanks should be recited upon going to the toilet.[3]

Here is my version based on the original Hebrew:

Wondrous is YHVH, the Happening happening as
all happening
Who manifests this body of marvelous balance and
complexity.
I am grateful for openings that open and closings
that close
All in tune with need and necessity.
If openings should close or that which is closed
open improperly,
I could not endure.
May I remember to honor this body
by respecting its form and function in all that I do.

[3] Talmud, Berachot 60b.

• CHAPTER 19 •

HOW TO VOTE

I once asked a Zen teacher if Buddhism had an ethical principle that could be a guide to voting in political elections. Yes, she said: "Minimize suffering and maximize happiness for all beings. Vote for people and policies that service these ends." She then pointed me to the Tevijja Sutta, the Sutra of the Threefold Knowledges where I found the Four Immeasurables:

> May all beings have happiness and the causes of happiness.
> May all beings be free from suffering and the causes of suffering.
> May all beings rejoice in the well-being of others.
> May all beings live in peace, free from greed and hatred.

Not long after, I shared this insight with my rebbe, Zalman Schachter-Shalomi, and asked him if he could provide me with something equally powerful and pithy from Judaism. He told me to stand up on one foot. When I did, he said, "What is hateful to you, don't do to anyone else. All politics should be commentary on this. Now go complicate it!"

Reb Zalman was playing with the teaching of Hillel who, when asked by a Roman soldier to teach the entire Torah while the soldier stood on one foot said, "What is hateful to you, do not do to another. All the rest is commentary. Now go and study it."[1] I loved and agreed with his notion that all politics should be rooted in Hillel's Golden Rule, but I was confused as to what he meant by "complicate it."

When I asked him to explain, he just said I would figure it out in time. I think I did. The more I investigated a politics of the Golden Rule the more complex my thinking became. Complex rather than complicated. Here is where my turning of Hillel has led me: the politics of Jewish Mind is about placing limits on power and the powerful. Here are six examples from Torah.

Limiting the Power of God. Abraham challenges God's plan to destroy Sodom saying, "How dare you kill the innocent along with the guilty! Should not the judge of all the earth deal justly?"[2] Abraham then teaches God what it means to be just by convincing God to spare the city if only ten righteous citizens reside there assuming, incorrectly as it turned out, that his nephew Lot, and Lot's wife, daughters, and sons-in-law would be the saving ten. This story and that of Akhnai's oven explored in Chapter Five, are examples of limiting the power of God.

Limiting the Power of the Chieftains. Torah strips tribal chieftains of judicial power by establishing a court system run by judges of sterling character who cannot be bribed by the chieftains.[3] In cases where the judges are unclear when rendering judgment,

---

[1] Talmud, *Shabbat* 31a.
[2] Genesis 18:25.
[3] Deuteronomy 16:19.

they are to consult with the priests and the chief justice, [4] but not with tribal chieftains or God.

Limiting the Power of Kings. When it comes to the power of royalty, Torah is explicit: "Don't trust the princes."[5] The early rabbis are even clearer: "Beware of the government, for rulers befriend you only for their benefit."[6] Torah allows the people to establish a king for themselves, but greatly restricts the power of the king.

> You may choose one from your community as king…but he must not acquire many horses for himself or return the people to Egypt in exchange for more horses… and he may not acquire many wives for himself… nor may he enrich himself with silver and gold.[7]

These limits are not arbitrary: limiting the king's ability to amass large herds of horses, especially much–prized Egyptian horses used to pull chariots, supply wagons, and other military hardware, limits the king's ability to advance his military agenda; limiting the number of wives a king could have limits the king's power since marrying into the royalty of other nations was the way kings sealed treaties with those nations and grew their influence and power.

Limiting the Power of the Priesthood and Levites. Torah limits the power of the priests and Levites by making them landless in a civilization that is almost completely dependent on farming for its survival.

---

[4] Deuteronomy 17:9.
[5] Psalms 146:3.
[6] *Pirke Avot* 2:3.
[7] Deuteronomy 17:14–20.

> The priests, the whole tribe of Levi, shall have no allotment or inheritance within Israel. They may eat the sacrifices that are the portion of YHVH, but they shall have no inheritance among the other members of the community; YHVH is their inheritance, as he promised them.[8]

The priests and Levites cannot grow their own food nor raise their own cattle. They are entirely dependent on the sacrifices the people bring to the Temple meaning that the very survival of the priestly system, not to mention the priests and Levites themselves, is dependent upon the will of the people. If the priests and Levites cease to meet the needs of the people, and the people cease to bring their sacrifices to the Temple, the entire priestly edifice falls. Despite all the pomp and pageantry of priesthood, the power lies with the people.

Limiting the Power of the Financial Elites. According to Joshua Berman in his book, *Created Equal: How the Bible Broke with Ancient Political Thought*, in the Ancient Near East,

> A peasant—a small landowner—resides on a small plot of privately owned lands and engages in subsistence farming. As his margins of profit are slim, he can go into debt for any number of reasons: personal illness, crop failure, taxation, or the monopoly of resources by the state or private elite. His first line of recourse is to procure a loan, which he can only get at high interest. The high interest renders him insolvent, so he is forced to sell or deliver family members into debt–slavery, to pay off the debt. When this does not secure the means to pay off the

[8] Deuteronomy 18:1–2.

debt, he has to resort to relinquishing or selling this own land—his means of production—and, finally to selling himself.[9]

The primary economic engine of the time was the family farm, and Torah sets forth a series of laws to protect it by limiting the power of wealthy landlords to gain permanent ownership of it.

First, Torah takes on the usurpation of land by wealthy elites by denying land ownership to any human, and placing it in the hands of God alone: "All the earth is Mine;"[10] "The earth is YHVH's and everything in it;"[11] "Behold the sky and the heavens beyond the sky belong to YHVH your God, as well as the earth and all that is found upon her."[12]

Second, a family farm cannot be sold in perpetuity and must be returned to the family on the jubilee,[13] about which I will have more to say in a moment.

Third, clans are obligated to support members who have lost their land, their homes, and their livelihoods, and extended family members are prohibited from profiting off the suffering of the distressed family by loaning them money at interest or selling them food at a profit.[14]

And fourth, even if things get so bad for a family that they have to sell themselves to other family members as slaves, they are not to be enslaved but are to be treated as hired servants and released from their servitude on the jubilee at which time "they

---

[9] Joshua Berman, *Created Equal: How the Bible Broke with Ancient Political Thought* (Oxford University Press, 2008), 87.
[10] Exodus 19:5.
[11] Psalm 24:1.
[12] Deuteronomy 10:14.
[13] Leviticus 25:29–31.
[14] Leviticus 25:35–38.

and their children shall be free from your authority; they shall return to their own family and their ancestral property."[15]

Not every family is going to fall into financial hardship, of course, so Torah adds a series of laws limiting what successful farmers can do with their land. For example, the Book of Leviticus restricts the ability of farmers to lay claim to the entirety of their seasonal harvest.

> When you reap the harvest of your land, you may not reap to the very edge of your fields, nor may you reclaim any of the harvest dropped by your workers. These you must leave for the poor and the foreigners living among you.[16]

Chapter 25 of Leviticus introduces the injunction of the sabbatical year placing far more drastic limits on the farmer. Torah demands that once every seven years the earth is to lay fallow and no farming shall be done at all. During the sabbatical year the farmer is prohibited from sowing fields or pruning vineyards: "the land is to have a year of rest."[17]

The farmer is further prohibited from harvesting for profit anything that grows of itself in the fields and vineyards,[18] and is obligated to use that produce to feed not only his family, but also

> male and female servants, and the hired worker and temporary resident who live among you, as well as your livestock and the wild animals in your land. Whatever the land produces may be eaten.[19]

[15] Leviticus 25:39–41.
[16] Leviticus 23:22.
[17] Leviticus 25:5.
[18] Leviticus 25:5.
[19] Leviticus 25:4–7.

No one is to go hungry during the sabbatical year, but no one is to make a profit either. Immediately after this limitation of the power of the farmer over farmland, Torah speaks of a jubilee year that falls once every seven sabbatical years:

> And you shall hallow the fiftieth year and you shall proclaim liberty throughout the land to all its inhabitants. It shall be a jubilee for you: you shall return every one of you to your property and every one of you to your clan.[20]

The year of jubilee is a time of resetting the economic balance scales. Given the contingencies of life as a subsistence farmer, artisan, or small business owner there is no way to prevent economic inequality from emerging, but the jubilee year places a two-generation limit on its impact. If your grandparents were forced to sell the family farm, and if they were forced by necessity to sell themselves and your parents into debt-servitude the jubilee means that this horror could not last more than forty-nine years and that you would be freed from debt and your family farm would be returned to you. Again, all of this harkens back to the principle that God rather than people owns the earth: "The land shall not be sold in perpetuity, for the land is Mine; with Me you are all aliens and tenants."[21]

The politics of Jewish Mind is a politics of limiting power. When I look at the world today, I don't see this ideal in play anywhere, including the State of Israel.

Generally speaking, we humans have replaced the quest for justice with the quest for power. We have made a fetish of the state and allowed xenophobia to poison our policymaking.

---

[20] Leviticus 25:10–11.
[21] Leviticus 25:23.

We have infected the idea of the homeland with the disease of empire. We have replaced our skepticism of power with a lust for power, and our suspicion of government with a passion for control. We have allowed the pain of the past to define who we are in the present and erase our hope of becoming something better in the future. This saddens me, but I am heartened by the ideal itself.

So, how do we vote when we vote from Zen Mind/Jewish Mind? We vote to limit power and the powerful in service to minimizing suffering and maximizing happiness for all beings.

· CHAPTER 20 ·

HOW TO DIE

Organized religion is built around death—rather, around our desperate and futile attempt to avoid death. Indeed, if we were immortal, we'd probably never invent religion in the first place. Since we're not, we do the next best thing and invent fantasies about heaven (for us) and hell (for them) or rebirth in this world or some other world—just so long as wherever we go after we are gone it is always us who goes there.

Who you are after you die must be the same "you" you were before you died otherwise none of the standard afterlife scenarios make sense. For example, there is no point in rewarding you in heaven if the "you" being rewarded isn't the "you" you imagine yourself to be here on earth. Or if reincarnation is more to your liking, if the "you" who is reborn isn't the "you" who died, then "you" aren't reborn at all. It is all about you or rather the "you" you imagine yourself to be. In other words, it is all about narrow mind.

In her book, *Naked in the Zendo*, Zen teacher and clinical psychologist Grace Schireson tells the story of choosing an urn to contain her cremation ashes when she died. Her husband bought it for her as a birthday gift. Once she received the urn, she writes, "I began to think about my afterlife in this gorgeous urn…. [W]ould I fit in the urn?… Would I be comfortable in the urn?… What if I died at sea [and could not be cremated]?… I began to realize the foolishness of my cravings. I wasn't actually using the urn to prepare for my death. I was attempting to both control and deny the end of my life as I knew it."[1]

Whether fretting over an urn or an afterlife fantasy, the lesson, as Grace Schireson writes, is the same: "I could not control my death, but I could live fully, with gratitude and acceptance. And at the time of death, I could face death with the same state of mind."[2]

I offer two prayers to help cultivate Zen Mind/Jewish Mind as death draws near. The first is adapted from the traditional Jewish *Viddui* or deathbed confession. The second is one I wrote inspired by the *Tibetan Book of the Dead*.

You can read the Viddui for oneself, or have it read on your behalf by a loved one. You can, of course, read it on behalf of another as well. In any case the text should be read slowly, mindfully, pausing after each verse to contemplate what has been read.

> I acknowledge before the source of all that life and death are not in my hands.
>
> Just as I did not choose to be born, so I do not choose to die.
>
> May it come to pass that I may be healed, but if death is my fate, then I accept it with dignity and the loving calm of one who knows the ways of all things.

[1] Grace Schireson, *Naked in the Zendo* (Shambhala, 2019), 156-57.
[2] Schireson, *Naked in the Zendo*, 159.

> May my death be honorable and my life be a
> healing memory for those who know me.
> May my loved ones think well of me and may
> my memory bring them joy.
> From all I may have hurt, I ask forgiveness,
> upon all who have hurt me, I bestow forgiveness.
> As a wave returns to the ocean, so I return to
> the source from which I came.
> *Shalom, shalom, shalom*; peace, peace, peace.[3]

I wrote the following to be read to the dying and the recently dead assuming that a modicum of self-conscious abides for a time even if one is pronounced dead. Even if this is not so, and even if the person to whom you are reading this text cannot hear you, I've been told by people who have read this text to loved ones that the benefit to the reader is powerful in and of itself.

Fix your attention on your beloved and read the words aloud slowly, pausing for the space of one complete breath between each verse. You may choose to substitute the name of your loved one for the generic "beloved."

> Listen, Beloved, and yield to the truth of what is
> happening. Trust my words. Rest in the sound of
> my voice. Be still and know that all is God.
> Listen, Beloved: you are not only the smaller
> self with its sensing, feeling, thinking, and doing;
> you are also the Greater Self beyond all sensing,
> feeling, thinking, and doing. You are not only the
> name you carry, but the Unnamed that carries
> you.

[3] Rabbi Rami Shapiro, *Last Breaths: A Guide to Easing Another's Dying* (Beth Or, 1993).

Listen, Beloved: you are to this world what a wave is to the ocean that waves it: a precious and never-to-be-repeated happening of the One happening as all happening.

Listen, Beloved: you are a way the One laughs and weeps and loves and suffers. You are a way the One knows itself as the many. You are a way the One knows itself as each part. And soon you will be a way the part comes to know itself as the One. You are becoming what you have always been: the nondual Aliveness forever birthing and dying.

Listen, Beloved: you have had many experiences in life. Some matched your desires, others did not; some fulfilled your goals, others did not; some upheld your values, others did not. Some brought you great joy, others brought you great suffering. These may arise in your mind as memories, reflections, yearnings, and regrets. Do not cling to what arises; only acknowledge the arising. Say "yes" to what was, without excuse or explanation.

Listen, Beloved: as you die, the faces of loved ones may come to you. Welcome each face with "I love you." Do not cling, excuse, or explain. Without clinging, excuse, and explanations there is only love.

Listen, Beloved: as you die, the faces of those you may have hurt may come to you. Welcome each face with "I am sorry." Do not cling, excuse, or explain. Without clinging, excuse, and explanation there is only forgiveness.

Listen, Beloved: as you die, the faces of those who may have hurt you may come to you. Welcome each face with "I understand." Do not cling, excuse, or explain. Without clinging, excuse, and explanation there is only peace.

Listen, Beloved: as you die, you may begin to forget, but you will not be forgotten. You may begin to let go, but you will not be abandoned. You may begin to drift, but you will never be set adrift. You are loved. I am here. You are not alone. You have never been alone.

Listen, Beloved: soon you may find yourself without moorings. This is because moorings are of the past, and you are entering the eternal Present. But you can still hear my voice. Attend to my voice. Trust my voice. Let my voice guide you.

Listen, Beloved: you are yielding to the One. Allow the One to draw you in. You may perceive the presence of others: some you know, some you don't. They are here to comfort you, as I am here to comfort you. Acknowledge them. Feel their love and welcome their support, but do not cling to them. They are here to honor your dying, but they have no place in your death. Let them come; let them go.

Listen, Beloved: the closer you get to the One, the lighter you will feel. You were a being; now you are *be*/ing itself. You were self-aware; now you are awareness itself. You were happy and sad; now you are only bliss.

Listen, Beloved: my voice may be fading. My love is not. Let me release you with this prayer:

> May you be free from fear. May you be free from compulsion.

May you be blessed with love. May you be blessed with peace.

You were loved. You are loved. You are love.[4]

---

[4] The question often arises if you can use these prayers for suicides. While there are religions that burden a person who commits suicide with judgment and sin, Judaism does not. The Jewish position is that the person who commits suicide does so under duress and is not responsible for their actions. Hence no sin is accrued. Compassion not judgment for the dead and the bereaved is all that is due. See Joseph Caro, *Shulchan Aruch*, Yoreh Deah.

· AFTERWORD ·

ZEN MIND/JEWISH MIND

Zen Mind:
Meet the Buddha. Kill the Buddha.

Jewish Mind:
Met the Buddha? Killed the Buddha? Call Kornfield,
Salzberg, and Cohen, Attorneys at Law.

ACKNOWLEDGMENTS

I hate the author's acknowledgment pages: "Writing takes a village…;" "I could not have written this book without the loving support of blah, blah, blah." I wrote this book all by myself. I am beholden to no one. Not Johannes Gutenberg for inventing the printing press, or Steve Jobs for inventing the Mac, or the Chinese for inventing paper, or my parents and teachers for inventing me, or my tireless and tirelessly upbeat agent Scott Edelstein, or my brutally honest first readers Frank Levy and Aaron Shapiro, or Paul Cohen, Jon Sweeney, Anne McGrath, Colin Rolfe and the other wonderful people at Monkfish Publishing, or my wife who would let me work for hours uninterrupted at my desk, or my Goldendoodle Sofiyah who would not, or Leonard Cohen who, being dead, probably doesn't care, or Professor Unno who, though also being dead, is probably still disappointed in me. Beholden or not, my love and my thanks to you all.

ABOUT THE AUTHOR

Rami Shapiro is an award-winning author of over thirty-six books on religion and spirituality. Rami received rabbinical ordination from the Hebrew Union College–Jewish Institute of Religion and holds a Ph.D. from Union Graduate School. Rabbi Rami co–directs One River Foundation (oneriverfoundation. org), writes the foundation's newsletter, *Ask Rabbi Rami*, and is contributing editor for *Spirituality & Health* magazine (spiritualityhealth.com) where he writes the advice column *Roadside Assistance for the Spiritual Traveler*. Rami can be reached via his websites: rabbirami.com and oneriverfoundation.org/.

www.ingramcontent.com/pod-product-compliance
Lightning Source LLC
Jackson TN
JSHW081106161224
75380JS00002BA/2